Turkish DELIGHTS to APPLIQUÉ

LINDA M. POOLE

American Quilter's Society
P. O. Box 3290 • Paducah, KY 42002-3290
www.AQSquilt.com

Located in Paducah, Kentucky, the American Quilter's Society (AQS) is dedicated to promoting the accomplishments of today's quilters. Through its publications and events, AQS strives to honor today's quiltmakers and their work and to inspire future creativity and innovation in quiltmaking.

EDITOR: BARBARA SMITH

GRAPHIC DESIGN: ELAINE WILSON

ILLUSTRATIONS: WILLIAM POOLE ILLUSTRATION/PROTEK PATENTS OF MILFORD, PENNSYLVANIA

COVER DESIGN: MICHAEL BUCKINGHAM

PHOTOGRAPHY: CHARLES R. LYNCH

Library of Congress Cataloging-in-Publication Data

Poole, Linda M.

      Turkish delights to appliqué / by Linda M. Poole.

          p. cm.

      ISBN 1-57432-788-7

      1. Quilting--Patterns.   I. Title.

TT835 .P643 2002

746.46'041--dc21

                    2001008432

Additional copies of this book may be ordered from the American Quilter's Society, PO Box 3290, Paducah, KY 42002-3290, or online at www.AQSquilt.com.

Dedication

This book is dedicated to my parents, Gero and Gloria Grohs, to my husband, William A. Poole, and my sister, Lorraine. Thank you a million times over for being the most extraordinary kind souls that you are. I love you all dearly.

In addition, this is a special dedication to my fifth grade teacher, Miss Meredith McDermott, who always told me that I would write a book someday. Thank you for encouraging and believing in me at such an impressionable age.

Contents

Acknowledgments

There comes a time when one discovers that we simply cannot do everything by ourselves. With all of my heart, I want to thank each and every person who has traveled this wonderful journey with me.

Rose Hahn opened a new world of appliqué to me with the simple use of a glue stick.

Gero Grohs, my dad, traveled to Istanbul, Turkey, to meet up with me after I had finished teaching in Ankara on my first trip to Turkey. It was so exciting to experience the first time we laid eyes on the mosques with their towering minarets sprinkled along the skyline. When I was a little girl, Dad never blinked an eye when I told him I wanted to be an artist when I grew up. How could he, he is the most talented artist and silversmith I know.

Gloria Grohs, my mother and best friend, gave me my first scissors at an early age and taught me embroidery and handwork, along with her mother, my loving Grandmother Margherita Peruzzi. Thank you, Mom, for your unconditional love and support and for always smiling when I asked for the hundreds of little favors. I am so happy we traveled and experienced the wonders of Istanbul together on my second trip there. Your appliqué work is truly outstanding and beautiful.

William Poole, my husband, is a talented artist and the love of my life. Bill has taught me that I can achieve anything I want to do. His support and input have been invaluable to me. I am even impressed with the appliqué lingo he has acquired! He has generously shared his own talents and art staff to help with the illus-

trations in this book...a big thanks to William Poole Illustration/Protek Patents of Milford, Pennsylvania.

The Milford Valley Quilters Guild of Milford, Pennsylvania, are my dearest friends and my greatest support system. How lucky I am to have all of you in my life.

Gunsu Gungor is my sweet and cherished friend from Ankara, Turkey. Our friendship is what sparked my curiosity about the Turkish arts and her beautiful country. Without her, this book would never have been born – she gave me my very first Turkish tiles.

Istemihan Talay, Turkish minister of culture, enthusiastically formed the first International Quilt Exhibition, with Gunsu Gungor and the Ministry of Culture. I am grateful for your invitation to teach, exhibit, and experience this life-altering journey in Ankara, Turkey.

Bonnie Browning, of Paducah, Kentucky, and JoAnn and Nick Musso from Dallas, Texas, traveled with me on my first visit to Turkey for the "Peace with Quilts Exhibition." Bonnie has quite a sense of humor and enjoys new things with child-like wonderment. You never know when Bonnie may be photographing your food. She taught me to look at a plate of food differently and more artistically. JoAnn can easily replace any self-help book on the shelf. She is the most realistic, honest person I know and has a true zest for life. When I see lavenders and purples, I instantly think of JoAnn. Nick has become my "Texas Dad" with my own Dad's blessings. He is a true gentleman and a kind soul, whom I will always cherish.

Carol Hill and Helen Umstead journeyed with Mom and me to Istanbul. I am indebted to these two creative ladies for spending late nights brainstorming with me and for their invaluable advice. Their artistic talent goes beyond words, and I thank them for their serious efforts on their outstanding quilts. What fun we all had laughing, learning, teaching, and making new friendships!

Judy Brumbaugh enthusiastically supported me from the very start of this endeavor. I have treasured our long walks in the mornings and just talking about life and quilting. I thank you for always taking the time to talk and teach me invaluable little tips to make my projects go more smoothly.

Bonnie McCaffery encouraged me along this wonderful journey. She has taught me how to persevere and focus. Her words of confidence have helped me go farther than I ever thought I could.

Susan Leighty, Diane Brush, Nancy Morgan, Arlene Santora, Susan Caldwell, Mary Ann Gosch, Leslie Lacika, Laura Orben, Barbara Anderson, Emmie Lyle, Tootsie Schroeder, Lillian Angus, Betty Rigo, Irma Stichling, and Kathy Oehlmann, thank you all so much for saying yes with no hesitation when I asked if you would lend your expertise in appliqué and piecing for this book. I could never have done this without you.

Rebecca Leighty, you may have only been in kindergarten, but those stitches you put into all the little pincushions I took to Turkey will someday soon turn into perfect appliqué stitches.

Judy Irish is the most talented long-arm quilter and artist I know. You have made my pieces dance with thread. I am indebted to your creativity.

Selma Agalar, my friend from Turkey, thank you for the opportunity to teach at your quilt association and to participate in the Kirkpare 2000 quilt show in Istanbul. Your encouragements and sweet smiles warm my soul.

Mr. Selim Bernardette, my Turkish friend, I cherish our correspondence and am indebted to your positive points of view.

To my mom-in-law Audrey Shope Weber and sis-in-law Billie Jo Poole, thank you for every encouraging word that stayed within me every step of the way; friend Holly Aschoff, who kept me giggling, laughing, and grounded on the "cloudy" days as well as the "sunny" ones, and friend Dr. Parimal Bhayana for offering me her smiles, genuine hugs, and inner strength that have given me my own strength; and John and Mary Murray, who traveled to Turkey for the Peace with Quilts Exhibition and carried all my breakable plates, with their precious designs, back home to the U.S.A. for me.

To Barbara Smith, my editor, friend, and "birthing coach" for this book. It was a pure pleasure working with you and learning that we could finish one another's sentences in conversation. I thank you with all my heart.

To all the wonderful people at the American Quilter's Society, thank you for believing in me and always being so cheerful and positive. You have made me feel like part of your family, even though I don't have a Kentucky accent.

Thank you to the needle, fabric, thread, and crystal companies for making products that make my quilts come to life and sparkle.

Preface

There are so many wonderful and beautiful things that I love and enjoy doing in my life. I love to cook, kiss my kitties, girl-talk, write, dance, hear a good joke, listen to music, write letters, draw, give hugs, and read everything I can get my hands on. The list could go on, but some of my most favorite things would be traveling, gardening, and...you guessed it...appliqué and quilting.

My love for needle and thread began at an early age. Weaving little potholders, knitting crooked scarves, cross-stitching various items, and crocheting afghan squares kept me busy through my young years. Then, as a young adult, I married Bill, a wonderful and talented artist, who filled my life with love and support.

One day, when I went to a new fabric store, on the wall hung a stunning sampler quilt with a sign-up sheet for a six-week course. I signed up for the class, met wonderful people, and had a new obsession that is still a focal point in my life after almost 14 years.

Four years after I learned to quilt, we moved to the hills of northeastern Pennsylvania. This is where my love for flowers flourished. I am in love with the changing seasons. The winter months mysteriously quiet my soul and give me time to quilt. Spring rejuvenates my mind.

I've traveled a lot in my life, partly because my parents took me and my younger sister, Lorraine, on wonderful camping vacations all over the United States. We also went to Europe to visit our relatives. I always felt blessed that Dad was from northern Germany and that Mom had her northern Italian heritage. It was a thrilling, exciting adventure to visit distant cities, listen to different languages, and sit in the art studio of my German grandparents, Emma and Hans Fridrich Grohs.

Now as an adult, when I travel, each country's culture, cuisine, artwork, and scenery inspire me. One year, Mom and I took a trip to a quilt exposition in Austria, where I met a wonderful Turkish quilter, Gunsu Gungor. Our love for quilting led to an exchange between her quilting students and my quilt guild, the Milford Valley Quilters. Our friendship led to an invitation from the Minister of Culture, Istemihan Talay, to teach and exhibit in Turkey at Ankara's first international Peace with Quilts Exhibition.

I was intrigued with the country. When I entered Topkapi Palace, I fell in love with the exquisite marble pillars, stonework, gardens, jewels, pottery, and archways. My heart fluttered when I saw my first authentic Iznik tiles. I instantly knew I wanted these most beautifully inspiring tiles to be the focus of my quilts, and I wanted to be able to share them with others.

The next time you travel, whether it be to an exotic island, on a drive in the countryside, or as a visit to a bustling city, let yourself be inspired. Perhaps you will find new color palettes or integrate a new quilt design from an interesting element you saw, or you may just start designing your own pieces of art!

Enjoy the journey!

Linda with Turkish quilter.

Iznik Tiles & Pottery

Millions of tourists every year travel to Turkey and are mesmerized by the beauty and art of hand-painted Turkish ceramics and tiles. These ceramics adorn the palaces of the sultans and the multitudes of mosques built by the emperors of the Ottoman period, especially the well-known Blue Mosque in Istanbul. It magnificently dazzles our eyes with some 20,000 tiles. There are also innumerable fountains that decorate the streets and courtyards all over the cities and small towns.

Flowers, such as tulips, pomegranates, roses, carnations, and blossoming spring trees were a dominant inspiration for the court artists in their designs for the tile makers in Iznik, a town known for pottery and tile making. The town became of vital importance with the cap-ture of Constantinople by the Ottomans in 1453. New palaces and dwellings were constructed along with many religious buildings.

The wealth of the ruling class created the need for tiles and pottery for the new establishments, and the kilns in Iznik became vitally important to the Imperialists. Toward the sixteenth century, naturalism became popular, and in Ottoman Turkish art, flowers were a most popular subject. Roses and hyacinths represented the splendor of the heavens above. "Lale," the Turkish word for tulip, became a repeatedly used motif. The colors used in the pottery, cobalt blue, emerald green, turquoise, and red, were inspired by semi-precious stones.

It was a most amazing experience to walk along the palace walls and see these tiles proudly shining in the light streaming though the arched windows. The tiles were visible not only on walls, but on fireplaces, niches, and recesses used for lamps. I visited many palaces and residences, along with an exciting visit to the Grand Bazaar in Istanbul, and met a most delightful tile manufacturer. He believes his art is necessary to bring the history of tiles into the modern day. Turkey has a most fascinating history, along with some of the most impressive pottery, tile, jewelry, sculpture, silver, fashion, and needlework.

I easily fall in love with each country I travel to or read about. It is amazing to learn and see just how much we have in common with one another. Our dreams, hopes, fears, and stories are parallel, even though we may not live on the same continent. These are the ideas that give me the curiosity to travel and see what our big world is all about. Perhaps one day, I will see you on a plane, train, or boat heading to a place where dreams happen.

Examples of Iznik ceramics.

Introduction

Grab your favorite cup of java, put your feet up, and enjoy the journey you are about to take. The treasures you will find and keep for life will include an easy-to-follow glue-stick method that allows you to join pieces together as units before appliquéing them to a background. These units make wonderful traveling projects.

You will also learn how to break out of the box by showcasing your work in easy-to-make large oval and circular backgrounds. In addition, you can easily adapt any of the flowers to several blocks, giving you the freedom to customize your quilts.

Begin with a simple pattern, such as the Starter Bouquet on page 32, then find yourself enticed to try a more challenging pattern. Have fun creating bouquets with a small or a large group of friends (see community projects on pages 29 and 30). Watch your vase overflow with colorful flowers.

Examples of Iznik pottery.

General Instructions

Choosing Supplies

We all sometimes learn from trial and error, but quality tools will certainly make the learning easier. Experiment and try new ones. You may find that a certain brand works better for you than another. The following is a list of things that make my appliqué a little easier. (For a list of resources, see page 126.)

Needles. Use a short needle to give yourself more control over your stitching. Try size 11 or 12 hand appliqué needles. Remember to change your needle often. A sharp point is the key to butter-smooth stitching. To make life easier when threading the tiny eyes of the needles, try a needle threader for both hand and machine needles.

Thimbles. Choosing a thimble is a matter of personal preference for each person. My choice is the little clear self-adhesive finger pads that last for hours at a time. You may need to try several styles of thimbles to find the one that works best for you.

Pins and pincushions. Pins come in many lengths and sizes, some with pretty colored glass heads, some without. Slender, small-diameter pins glide more easily into the fabric and keep the appliqué pieces flatter against the background fabric. Always have a strawberry pincushion close by. Periodically stick your pins and needles into the strawberry, which is filled with sand, to keep them sharp.

Scissors. It is wise to use three pairs of scissors, one for cutting fabric; another pair to cut anything other than fabric (paper, template plastic, etc.); and a pair of 4" embroidery scissors for cutting thread, small pieces of fabric, and tiny seam allowances. Scissors are essential tools, so invest in quality, and remember to always keep a sheath on the points to protect them. Keep your scissors in a special place so they are not misused for any other projects in the home.

Marking devices. Keep many different marking tools on hand. A mechanical pencil provides a consistent thin line, and a water-soluble blue pen washes out. Dressmaker's transfer paper and a tracing pen help eliminate the need for a light box or window for tracing. The paper comes in five colors and shows up well on dark fabrics.

Glue sticks. Water-soluble glue sticks are a must for the glue-stick appliqué method. Use a name brand made for fabrics so it will wash out. It is important to always re-cap the glue stick when you are finished using it so the glue doesn't dry out.

Freezer paper. There are two types of freezer paper on the market. One is a plain paper and the other is plastic coated. The preferred type is the plastic-coated one. Draw your appliqué shapes on the dull side. Place the plastic-coated side down on the fabric. Press the paper with a dry iron set on medium-hot. The freezer-paper will adhere to the fabric, which can be peeled off easily and reused.

Toothpicks or skewers. These little items are invaluable tools. Either will do the job well. They help turn under little unruly pieces that need a little taming. Use a skewer to ensure perfect points and curves.

Fusible interfacing. Use the lightweight fusible interfacing for the Large Circles method described on page 22.

Light box or window. For tracing your patterns, you can either buy a small light box or easily make one by placing tempered glass between two tables with a lamp underneath. Or, you can just tape your material to a clean window.

Thread. It is important to match your thread colors to your appliqué pieces as closely as possible. A mercerized cotton embroidery thread is a good choice. It comes in a wide array of colors, and if you cannot find a perfect matching color, use one shade darker rather than lighter.

Bias tape. For making stems, two choices are available. One is bias fusible tape. It comes in a nice selection of colors. The second tool is a bias-tape maker (described on page 20).

Fusible thread. When you want to sew down a meandering stem or anything else, you can either machine or hand sew a line of fusible thread on the background, then iron your stem or appliqué piece so that it adheres to the thread. It will then be in a stable position for you to appliqué.

Tweezers or bodkin. Either one of these tools can be used to remove freezer paper from the back of a sewn-down appliqué piece.

Other useful items.
Iron with a pointed tip
Ironing board or surface
Rotary cutter, mat, and ruler
Compass
Yardstick compass
Cardboard
Lamp
Pointer for turning curves

Traveling Supplies

If you too would like to travel overseas to find sources of inspiration for your quilts, here are some things you may want to take with you.

Notebook and pencil. Keep these for quick sketches, phone numbers, inspirations, and anything you need to remember.

Camera and film. Take a camera along for that perfect moment. Extra film is helpful, especially if you need to click a series of pictures and don't want to run out.

Tiny tripod. Using a tripod with your camera will let you photograph your subject matter without shaking. The tripod I own is so small, it fits in my briefcase.

Water. I find that, when I'm traveling, I dehydrate easily, and a bottle of water at my fingertips will prevent this.

Batteries. You will need them for your camera and flash, and if you own a voice-activated recorder. There is nothing worse than being inspired when the batteries are running out.

Foreign dictionary. This will be a lifesaver for the necessities like food and restroom. Sign language is always universal.

Small currency. Instead of pulling out all your money at one time, carry some small bills in a separate place. It's not necessary for everyone to see how much money you have, especially when you have no idea either, because you don't know the currency system. I keep small amounts in different pockets for purchasing a soda and sandwich or paying cab fare. Make sure you learn your foreign currency at least to the ability of buying a bottle of water.

Photographer's vest. This is one of the best purchases I've made for traveling. It has pockets for everything, and I found it can be worn for different seasons with an appropriate shirt underneath. Vests usually have a place for a bottle of water, passport money, film, and much more. For a woman, it eliminates the purse-carrying habit.

Business card from your place of lodging. If you ever are lost or need to direct a cab and cannot speak the language, just show the card and you will arrive at your destination.

Passport. Keep it on you at all times. It is essential to your existence. I also keep a photocopy of my passport in my luggage and at home.

Whistle on a chain. A whistle can be handy when you are traveling alone and are in the cities at night. Mom always says it is better to be safe than sorry!

Medication or vitamins
Don't forget to bring them.

Ice pack and aspirin. When I travel, I walk all day. In ancient cities, that means walking on uneven cobblestones, up and down hills, and winding around valleys. I always bring an ice pack with me and put it in the freezer at the hotel or a friend's place. It is surely welcome for my tootsies, ankles, or head at the end of the day, along with an aspirin.

Watch. A timepiece keeps me on schedule. Make sure to set it to the new time zone.

Journal. Include one if you like to record your experiences.

Address book. You will need one if you like to send postcards. I also keep entries of the people and places I will be visiting in a particular country. In addition, I enter all of the new addresses of the wonderful people I have met.

A smile. A smile is worth a thousand words, and it is a universal language. You'll know when to put on your "serious" face, but when I smile, I always get one back!

Selecting Fabric

COLOR

One invaluable lesson I've learned is to always wash my fabrics before doing anything. The reason for doing this is to prevent shrinkage, because the glue-stick method for appliquéing involves a warm soak at the end of the sewing to remove the freezer paper. In addition, some fabric dyes bleed slightly, which can ruin a beautiful piece.

Sort your fabrics by color families and wash them in warm water with pure soap. Transfer the fabrics to the dryer and pull them out before they are completely dry to prevent excessive wrinkling. Iron them dry and rub the darker fabrics against a white piece. If the color rubs onto the white, rewash the dark one until the bleeding stops. If it continues to bleed, do not use that piece.

Let's talk a little about fabrics and all the wonderful choices you have. Are you the type that practically bites your nails off when faced with picking fabrics for your next project? Do you cover your eyes and stick your hand into your stash hoping to pull out something decent to use? Or are you a person who can basically figure out a nice selection of colors that go together?

Everyone has a different method for choosing colors. I seem to pick my palettes depending on my mood for the day. To me, it's like drinking warm cocoa on a cold day or eating ice cream on a sweltering summer afternoon. You guessed it. I love to use warm and cool or hot and cold colors together in my quilts.

There is usually no rhyme nor reason for the first fabrics that I select. These are my jump-starters. They may have a color or certain design element that captures my eye. If you stand too long mulling over fabrics, you may become frustrated, and the project will no longer be fun. So, I strongly suggest that you just get some fabrics in your hands, and everything will usually fall into place.

BACKGROUNDS

When picking your background fabric, keep in mind that it will become the foundation for all the other colors that will join it. Try picking several different pieces. If the background is too busy with multitudes of colors and designs, there is a chance the appliquéd pieces will get lost, which will not do justice to all the work you have done. Subtle colors, blending and swirling in hand-dyed fabrics or anything similar, are wonderful choices (Fig. 1–1).

Fig. 1–1. Hand-dyed background fabrics.

Fig. 1–2. Sparkling background fabrics.

Fig. 1–3. Watercolor and marbled backgrounds.

Both bold or delicate background colors glistening with sparkles can offer a wonder feeling of excitement to a piece (Fig. 1–2).

Delicate watercolor or soft marble effects can add a feeling of soft romance and feminine appeal (Fig. 1–3).

An understated pattern provides a hint of interest to the background (Fig. 1–4).

STEMS AND LEAVES

Keep a wide variety of different shades of green in your stash, as well as other leaf-like colors. Having a wide array of colors will enable you to have a nice contrast to any background piece you may pick. Remember, no one says that a stem or leaf must be green (Fig. 1–5).

FLOWERS

Choosing colors for each flower is the best part of the project. Search for fabrics with little

Fig. 1–4. Understated background pattern.

accents of color: dots, swirls, and geometric patterns (Fig. 1–6). You can also cut interesting elements from novelty or scenic prints.

Whether you are shopping for fabric or looking through your own stash, take a double look at something you may think would never work in your design. Who would have thought that, by cutting and dissecting fish fabric, wonderful texture could be added. The possibilities are endless, so experiment and free yourself for a new venture.

Glue-Stick Appliqué

HAVE ON HAND:
Water-soluble glue stick
Water-soluble blue marker
Skewer or toothpick
Bodkin or tweezers
Background fabric
Fabric scraps for petals and flowers
Appliqué needles
Matching thread
Small piece of cardboard
Freezer paper
Iron
Warm water
Damp washcloth
Towel
Compass
Mechanical pencil
Paper scissors
Small embroidery scissors

OPTIONAL:
Light box
Transfer paper and tracing stylus

Fig. 1–5. Samples of greens for stems and leaves.

Fig. 1–6. Samples of flower fabrics.

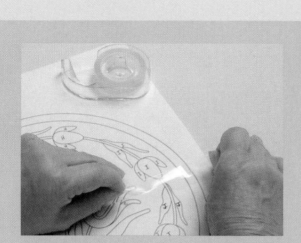

Fig. 1–7. Tape pattern sections together.

Fig. 1–8. Label each flower-leaf grouping.

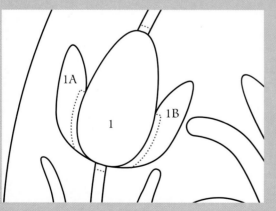

Fig. 1–9. Mark the open areas with dots.

MASTER COPY

On a photocopy machine, copy the pattern you want to make, or trace the pattern by hand on a sheet of freezer paper. Most patterns are given in sections. If you trace the sections on separate sheets of freezer paper, cut them on the dashed lines and tape them together to make a whole pattern, making sure the design lines match (Fig. 1–7).

Label each flower piece and leaf with its number-letter designation (Fig. 1–8).

FREEZER-PAPER TEMPLATES

Tape your master copy to a window or light box. Note that patterns are reversed from the images in the photos. The reversed templates will be pressed to the wrong side of the fabrics, so the pieces will be in the correct orientation when appliquéd.

Tape a piece of freezer paper, shiny side down, over the master copy. With a pencil or thin permanent marker, draw the entire pattern on the dull side of the freezer paper. Mark each flower piece and the leaves with the same number-letter combination that is on the master copy.

You will not need to label the bias stems, but trace them on the copy to use as placement guides. After drawing your pattern on the freezer paper and labeling each piece, you can untape the papers.

OVERLAPPING PIECES

Look at each flower closely and determine which pieces are on top of other pieces. A "closed" area is one that must have the allowance turned under before being appliquéd. An "open" area does not need to be turned because it will be covered by another piece. On the freezer-paper pattern, indicate the open and closed areas on each piece. You can indicate an open section by making little dots along the edge. Just think of the dots as little "o's" for the word "open" (Fig. 1–9).

With paper scissors, cut out the freezer-paper pieces on the drawn lines (Fig. 1–10). These pieces will be your templates for marking the appliqué fabrics.

CUTTING FABRIC PIECES

Place the freezer-paper templates shiny side down on the wrong side of the appropriate fabrics and press them for a few seconds with a dry, medium-hot iron (Fig. 1–11). Check to see that the freezer paper has adhered to the fabric.

Cut the fabric pieces with a ³⁄₁₆" turn-under allowance around each template. There's no need to measure the allowance. Just cut it by eye (Fig. 1–12).

Stopping just short of the turn line, clip the inside curves of the closed sections with your small embroidery scissors (Fig. 1–13, page 18).

TURNING ALLOWANCES

For gluing, use a piece of cardboard to keep the table surface clean. With the appliqué piece wrong side up, lightly apply glue on the allowances of the closed sections (Fig. 1–14, page 18). Turn the allowances and use a damp washcloth to wipe your fingers clean of glue residue.

Fig. 1–10. Cut out each freezer-paper piece.

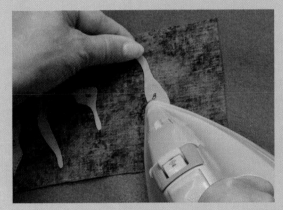
Fig. 1–11. Press templates on the wrong side of the fabric.

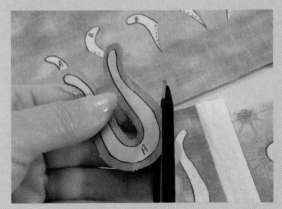
Fig. 1–12. Add turn-under allowances when cutting fabric pieces.

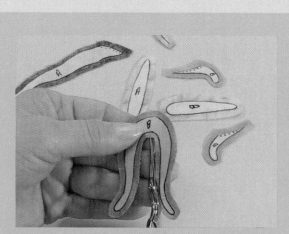

Fig. 1–13. Clip closed sections, if needed.

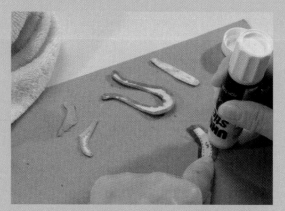

Fig. 1–14. Use a glue stick on closed sections.

Fig. 1–15. Glue-baste the pieces of a unit together.

SEWING UNITS

Decide which pieces need to be sewn together as a unit before being appliquéd to the background. Glue-baste the pieces together as follows: With the pieces wrong side up, lightly glue the wrong side of the fabric in the appropriate open sections. Hold the pieces up to a lamp or window to help with positioning and manually join the pieces (Fig. 1–15). Then appliqué the pieces together (Fig. 1–16). Continue adding pieces in this manner until the unit is complete.

PREPARING THE BACKGROUND

After your pieces have been appliquéd together into units, you are ready to prepare the background fabric.

Cut a square piece of background fabric at least a couple of inches larger all around than your pattern. Tape your master copy to a light box or window. (If the pattern is asymmetrical, place the pattern side facing toward the window so the image is reversed to match the photo.) Center the background fabric, right side up, on the pattern. Tape the fabric to the light box or window and, with a water-soluble blue marker, lightly trace the pattern on the fabric (Fig. 1–17). This tracing is a placement guide for the appliqué pieces.

Alternatively, you can use transfer paper and a tracing stylus. Tape your fabric, right side up, to a table. Tape the colored side of the transfer paper facing down. Tape your pattern down with the design facing downward. With the tracing stylus held vertically, apply pressure to trace the pattern. Periodically take a careful peek at your tracing to make sure you are

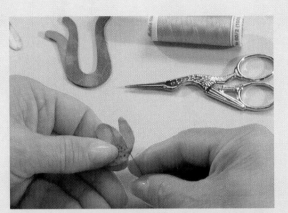

Fig. 1–16. Appliqué the unit pieces together.

Fig. 1–17. Trace the pattern on the background.

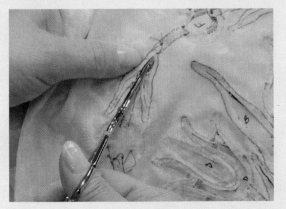

Fig. 1–18. Carefully cut away the background from under the appliqués.

Appliqué Tips and Tricks

A sharp needle is the key to making smooth stitches. There's more than one in a package, so don't try stretching the use of one needle for the entire project.

Keep your scraps of fabric from past projects. I am often amazed that a piece of fabric I have kept for years is the perfect accent to spice up a flower in a quilt. You can always trade off scraps with friends, too.

Try different glue sticks, but above everything, water-soluble glue is the ticket to getting the freezer paper off when you soak your appliqué in water. I like a glue stick that glides easily over the fabric when applied.

If you're not fond of basting with thread, try a spray-and-fix product. It gently adheres the fabric layers to one another and eliminates thread basting.

I use a table lamp whose bulb emits true colors. Not only does it shine with extra light, but I can see my stitches and colors better.

When appliquéing a piece with a deep curve or valley, take extra stitches to secure the sewing.

If your thread tangles a lot, either cut a shorter length or try pulling the thread through beeswax to help your thread glide through the fabrics more easily.

Put together a travel bag with all the necessary threads, needles, etc., to tote with you wherever you go, and your appliqué project will always be at your fingertips. I use a make-up travel tote that has zip pouches, pockets, and the do-dads that are perfect for me. Keep your eyes open, and you will find your own perfect little travel companion.

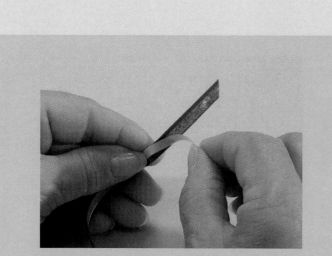

Fig. 1–19. Fusible bias tape.

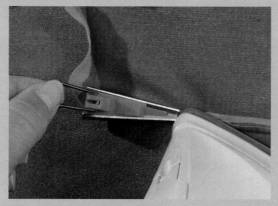

Fig.1–20. Bias-tape maker.

applying enough pressure. When you are finished, untape the "sandwich," and you will have an imprint of your design on the fabric.

APPLIQUÉING THE PIECES

Look at your pattern and determine which piece needs to be appliquéd first. Put a little dab of glue on the back to hold it in place for sewing and position the piece on the background. Appliqué around the edges. Then select the next piece or unit and appliqué it in place.

When all the pieces and units have been appliquéd, the background fabric can be cut away from underneath them. Leave a ³⁄₁₆" seam allowance of background fabric under the appliqués (Fig. 1–18, page 19).

BIAS STEMS

Fusible bias tape. There are two different methods for making stems. One simple way is to use pre-made, folded, fusible bias tape. (See resources on page 126). The tape comes in a large assortment of colors, and it is a piece of cake to use with its quick-release strip on the back (Fig. 1–19). Cut the length of tape needed for the project. Peel off the release tape and, with a dry medium-hot iron, press the tape on the fabric. It makes beautiful curves and is easy to miter. Appliqué down both sides by hand or machine.

Bias-tape maker. If you prefer, you can use a bias-tape maker (Fig. 1–20). This comes in many different sizes. The ¼" tape maker is suitable for stems. Cut ½" fabric strips on the bias. Insert one end of the strip into the tape maker and pull it through the little slit on top of the tool with a pin or awl. Then lightly pull just a little bit out of the other end. Pin the end to the ironing board and pull the tool to slide it down the strip. Press the folded strip as you pull the tape maker.

Bias Minder

When traveling to your quilt guild, sewing group, a class, or just about anywhere that requires you to take along bias tape, you may experience your freshly made tape becoming wrinkled. I have found a handy solution to that problem.

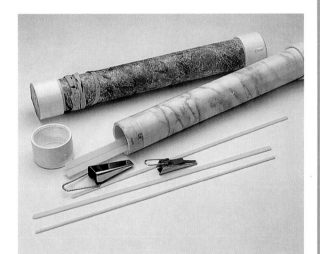

While at the local hardware store with my husband, I always peruse the aisles to see how I can adapt a "hardware thing" into my quilting life. When I discovered PVC pipe and caps to fit the ends, you would have thought I had won the lottery.

MATERIALS NEEDED

1. 2" plastic PVC pipe cut to any length suitable for your needs. Mine is 13" long. Many times, someone at the hardware store will cut any length you ask for.
2. Plastic PVC cap ends.
3. Sandpaper, to lightly sand the rough edges of the pipe.
4. Pretty contact paper, if you would like to cover the end caps and pipe.

Inside this tube, you can store your bias-tape makers, celtic press bars, pins, rolled fabric, small scissors, and tape. When you make bias tape for stems, simply wrap it around the tube and pin the end to keep it wrinkle-free, and it travels very nicely.

Fig. 1–21. Soak block in warm water.

Fig. 1–22. Remove the freezer paper.

Fig. 1–23. Roll appliqué in a towel to remove excess water.

REMOVING FREEZER PAPER

Dip the entire block in warm water for several minutes. Lightly agitate the block (Fig. 1–21)

Carefully remove the freezer paper from the appliquéd piece with the aid of a bodkin or tweezers, making sure not to puncture the fabric (Fig. 1–22).

PRESSING THE APPLIQUÉ

Lay the wet block flat on a towel. Roll the towel and the wet appliqué together. Gently squeeze to remove the excess water (Fig. 1–23)

Unroll the appliqué block and place it wrong side up on an ironing board covered with a towel. Use an iron on the cotton setting to gently press the piece dry. Be careful not to scorch the fabric.

Large Circles

After the piece has been appliquéd, if you like, you can turn the square block into a circle (see WHIRLING TULIPS, page 35). One of the best little tools for creating a large circle is the yardstick compass (Fig. 1–24). Use the yardstick compass to draw a circle the size needed on lightweight fusible interfacing. Cut the circle out, leaving about a ½" seam allowance or slightly more.

The interfacing has a slightly bumpy side that goes face down on the appliqué block which is face up. Center the circle on the block and press it lightly, gently, and quickly just to tack it in place. Sew completely around the circle on the pencil line and trim the seam allowances to ¼" (Fig. 1–25).

Cut a slit in the interfacing, not quite to the seam line, and turn the piece right side out. Use a pointer or another rounded end to slide into the slit and smooth out the seam. You are ready to sew your circle to another piece of fabric. Press the circle down and appliqué the edge to the second fabric.

Large Ovals

Large ovals are easy to draw. First, decide how long and wide you want your oval. Cut a strip of lightweight cardboard or template plastic that is an inch or two longer than half the oval's length. The strip, which will become your "ruler," can be about an inch wide.

Place a mark (A) near the left end of your cardboard or plastic "ruler." Referring to Fig. 1–26, the distance between A and C is half the length of the desired oval. The distance between B and C is half its width. Place the B and C marks on your ruler.

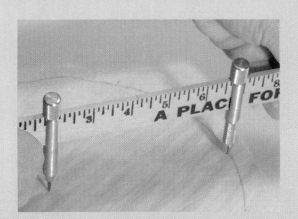

Fig. 1–24. Yardstick compass.

Fig. 1–25. Trim the seam allowances to ¼".

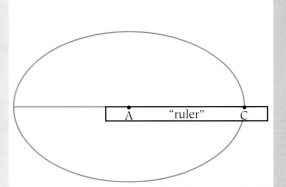

Fig. 1–26. A to C is half the desired oval's length. B to C is half the oval's width.

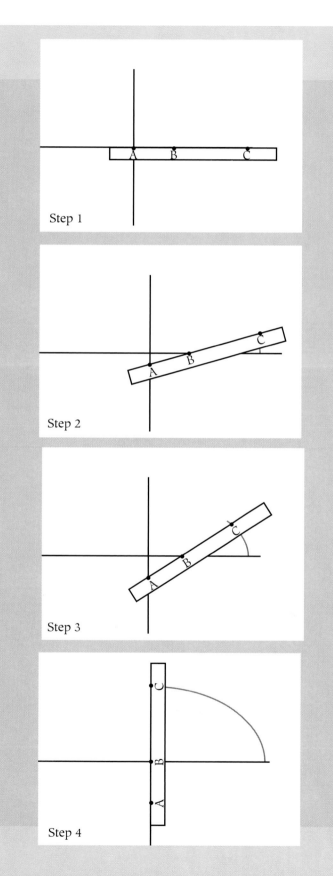

Step 1

Step 2

Step 3

Step 4

In the middle of a piece of paper, large enough to accommodate the oval, draw a line the length of the desired oval. At the center of the line, draw another line perpendicular to the first one for the oval's width.

Align your "ruler" as shown in Fig. 1-27 (Step 1) and place a mark on the paper at C. Move the A mark a short way down the vertical line and adjust B so it is on the horizontal line. Make another mark at C. Keeping A on the vertical line and B on the horizontal line, continue moving the ruler short distances and marking the oval at C.

When A, B, and C are aligned on the vertical line, you will have marked one fourth of the oval. Repeat the marking instructions for each quarter to complete the oval.

Alternatively, you can fold a sheet of paper into quarters and draw one quarter of the oval on the folded sheet as shown in Fig. 1-28. Cut the folded paper on the line. Unfold the paper to reveal the completed oval.

Quilting Ideas

Thought and consideration should be put into the quilting designs and process. It is like putting the finishing touches on your labor of love. Judy Irish, who owns and operates Wild Irish Rows in Arlington, Washington, lovingly quilted many of the gallery quilts and the samples in Figs. 1-29a-d, pages 25 and 26. When I asked her thoughts on machine quilting, Judy enthusiastically said, "Machine quilting is really not a mystery. You really can do it without suffering shoulder cramps and puckers in your quilt.

Fig. 1-27 LEFT. Moving A down the vertical line and B left along the horizontal line, mark the oval at C.

"Most local quilt shops have many classes available, or you can learn from the many wonderful books on the market. The main thing to remember is to have fun, don't take the machine too seriously, and remember that you are just quilting, not performing brain surgery.

"Some things to remember: If you are machine quilting, do pin basting and use a lot of pins. You should have two to four under the space of your hand, this will prevent puckers on the back of your quilt.

"Don't watch the needle, but look ahead to where you are going, just like driving your car!

"Have a vague idea in mind of what you want to quilt and just doodle all over the quilt. If you are a doodler, this is where you can put all those doodles to good use, and if you are not, now is the time to start.

"If you are a real beginner, use your walking foot to do straight lines. Remember that the straight lines can go in any direction and even cross over one another. You make the rules! Some students have done incredible curved lines with their walking-foot attachment. See what you can do.

"If you want to practice an easy method, simply trace the outline of the designs in your fabric, then you won't even have to mark your quilt or worry about a design. This is excellent practice for machine quilting.

"Look for inspiration everywhere in the world around you...on fabric, stationery, napkins, wallpaper, advertisements, or design books. The possibilities are endless and so much fun to discover. Let your piecing guide you with

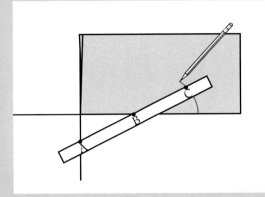

Fig. 1–28. Mark a quarter of the oval on a paper folded in fourths.

Fig. 1–29a. Quilting doodles by long-arm quilter Judy Irish.

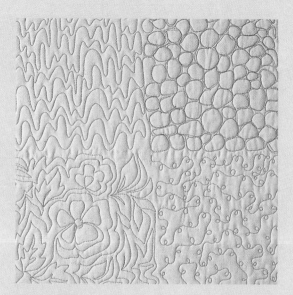

Fig. 1–29b.

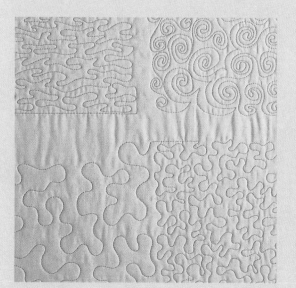

Fig. 1–29c.

Fig. 1–29d.

the designs, and if you are not perfectly happy with the results, just make another quilt. Machine quilting is like learning to do anything, you must practice, practice, practice. Have a great time and just think of the needle as your pencil and the quilt top as your paper. Have fun and be prepared to find a whole new world to explore with your needle and thread."

I find that all of Judy's inspirational ideas hold true for hand quilting too.

Embellishments

Either you're an embellisher or you're not, but once you start, you just can't stop. Your next trinket or treasure can easily be found at a garage sale or consignment shop. No guilty feelings there! Remember, we're on a mission to find the exact, perfect embellishment for this or any future quilt.

On the other hand, if garage sales aren't your thing and store shopping is, you now have a sense of purpose to hop into the car and go find just the right shades of beads and baubles, and if they are not there, then onward to the next store. Absolutely justifiable...right? Of course!

Embellishing provides the freedom to unleash your artistic side, especially if you have never designed an original pattern. The adornment of your finished patchwork project gives it your own personal touch.

An embellishment can be just about anything your imagination would like it to be...all colors, sizes, and shapes of beads, buttons, charms, laces, doilies, shells, stones, yarns, tassels, cording, ribbons, sequins, tulle, glitter, creative stitching, and whatever else you can find, Figs. 1–30.

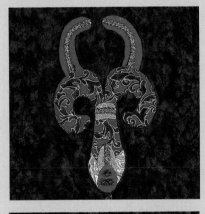

Figs. 1-30. Embellisment details from AUGUSTA'S GARDEN, full quilt shown on page 123.

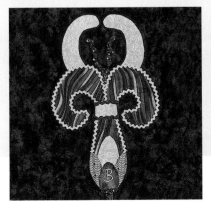

Progressive Quilt Bouquets

Whether you have a small group of four or a large group of 50, the Progressive Quilt Bouquet can get those creative juices flowing. Your group will enjoy the challenge and mystery of passing around a piece of fabric that eventually grows and blooms into a beautiful bouquet.

Your rules can be as simple or elaborate as you want them to be. The key to this project is to have fun, perhaps try something new, keep a secret (only if you want the end results to be a surprise), and pass the quilt to the next person on time.

The Milford Valley Quilters Guild of Milford, Pennsylvania (I am a very proud member of this group), graciously accepted my challenge for two Progressive Quilt Bouquets.

IN THE PINK and TRUE BLUE (pages 29 and 30) had simple guidelines passed with the quilt in a box. (An unused pizza box is perfect.)

The box contained the following items:
• A numbered sign-up list and a due date for passing the quilt to the next person.
• Four flower patterns.
• Background fabric with the vase drawn with a blue water-soluble marker. The drawing was included so people would know where to sew the bottoms of the stems.
• Pre-made bias tape was included, but participants could make their own.

There were only a handful of rules:
• For TRUE BLUE, the color scheme was blue, white, and cream.
• For IN THE PINK, the color scheme was green, pink, and purple.
• Participants could add to but not take from or cover another person's work.
• A participant could donate to the box a piece of fabric used for her flower. In turn, someone could use the fabric as an interesting accent piece for her own flower. This sharing of fabrics helped tie all the colors together in the block.

For your Progressive Quilt Bouquet, anything goes. Use any method of appliqué or embellishment you please. Have fun! Sign the enclosed label, and pass the box along on time.

To determine who gets the finished quilt, have everyone who worked on the quilt put his or her name in a hat and draw a winner. It has worked successfully in our guild for many years. We also display the quilt at our bi-annual quilt show. There, all can see how creative a diverse group of women of all ages can be. Quilters have no boundaries or differences when it comes to exercising their creativity.

Reflections

Have you ever given much thought to the happiness you feel when you have created something? It is a euphoric emotion that seems to generate a gentle rippling effect on others.

Quilters are wonderful, loving, kind, and caring people. We all have something to learn from and to teach one another.

I love appliqué, but as of this date, I cannot do needle-turn appliqué very well. I wanted to appliqué so badly, that I just found the method that suited my purposes, and this is what I hope for each one of you.

Never say never. There is always someone willing to show you a pointer or two or three.

Do whatever is needed to give your heart that joyous feeling of accomplishment, and then go teach someone what you learned and watch the ripple effect you started.

Thank you for the honor of letting me leave my soul-print in your library of books.

IN THE PINK, 39" x 48", by the Milford Valley Quilters Guild, of Pennsylvania: Lillian Angus, Diann E. Becker, Diane Brush, Susan Caldwell, Jeanne Green, Gloria Grohs, Carol A. Hill, Amelia Kroposki, Ellen Hetrick Kuber, Emmie Lyle, Helen P. Marinaro, Kathleen Porycki, Betty Rigo, Tootsie Schroeder, Irma Stichling, Denise Sweeney, Shirley Taddonio, and Helen Umstead.

TRUE BLUE, 33" x 33", by the Milford Valley Quilters Guild, of Pennsylvania: Barbara Anderson, Diann E. Becker, Marion Benson, Janet A. Churchill, Laura Decker, Laura deGraaf, Marie B. DiGerlando, Jane C. Fialcowitz, Mary Ann Gosch, B.J. Herter, Leslie Lacika, Carol Lawrence, Emmie Lyle, Mary McDowall, Ginnie Moore, Mary Murray, Laura M. Orben, Patti Shreiner, Kathy Snyder, Barbara Staskowski, Helen Umstead, and Catherine Wells.

Block Patterns

Appliqué Techniques

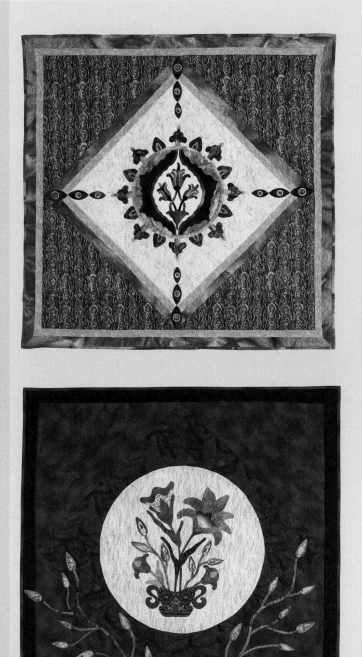

CAT'S EYE (TOP RIGHT), 39" x 39". Hand appliquéd and pieced by the author; machine quilted by Judy Irish, Arlington, Washington. Cotton floss was used to fancy stitch around the inner circle. Each circle appliquéd within the cat's eye is a swirling design element from the main background piece.

SUN DANCE (BOTTOM RIGHT), 42½" x 42½". Hand appliquéd and pieced by the author; machine quilted by Judy Irish, Arlington, Washington. The vase contains a selectively cut design in the center. Happy, soft, colors are used to uplift the spirit. The circle is appliquéd to a block set on-point, then wrapped at the bottom with growing vines and buds.

Starter Bouquet

STARTER BOUQUET block by Laura M. Orben.

STARTER BOUQUET quilt (CLOSE-UP) by Diane Brush.

STARTER BOUQUET block by Barbara Anderson.

STARTER BOUQUET block by Emmie Lyle.

W̲hen first learning to appliqué, I was always intimidated by the patterns in magazines and books. Naturally, my curiosity got the better of me, and I eventually learned to visually dissect the patterns. I created STARTER BOUQUET to enable you to pick any flower from these pages to create a simple bouquet if you want to practice the techniques, or a complex one if you have more experience. Because the patterns are not all the same size, you may want to use a photocopier to enlarge or reduce the stems and flowers to please yourself.

A great example of using different flowers to create a bouquet can be seen in the two progressive quilts, IN THE PINK (page 29) and TRUE BLUE (page 30).

Finished block: 15" x 15"

Fabrics and supplies

Flowers: assorted scraps
Bias stems: 36" bias tape ¼" wide
    (instructions, page 20)
Stem ring: 3" x 3"
Background: 17" x 17"
Freezer paper: two pieces 17" x 17"

Preparation

Please read the General Instructions, beginning on page 10, before starting your project.

1. Trace the pattern (page 34) on the dull side of one of the 17" freezer-paper squares. It will be your master copy for the stems. Use the other piece for making templates for the stem ring and the flowers of your choice (see Flowers, step 7). Lightly trace the master copy on the 17" background fabric square.

2. Make a freezer-paper template for the stem ring. Press the template shiny side down on the back of the appropriate fabric.

3. Cut the fabric stem ring, adding a ³⁄₁₆" turn-under allowance by eye as you cut. Then turn under the allowance. To make the center opening of the stem ring, slit the center side to side and turn under the edges.

Block assembly
STEMS

4. Cut the bias tape into three 12" lengths. Lay the stems on the background, crossing them as shown in the pattern. Appliqué the edges from the bottom to the stem-ring position.

5. Gently slip the tops of the stems through the opening in the stem ring (Fig. 2–1). Lift the stem ring and apply a light coating of glue under the edges.

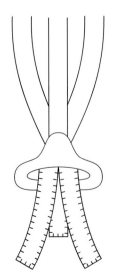

Fig. 2-1. Appliqué the lower part of the stems, then add the stem ring.

6. Lightly press the ring in place. Adjust the free ends of the stems so they lie flat. Appliqué the stem ring and the rest of the stems.

FLOWERS

7. Choose three flowers from any pattern in the book and enlarge or reduce them as needed. (Flowers that fit in a 3" square would make a good size.) Follow each pattern's directions for making flower units.

8. Appliqué a flower over the end of each stem. Cut the background fabric from behind the appliqué, leaving a ¼" allowance.

Finishing

9. Soak the block in warm water and remove the freezer paper. When the block is nearly dry, place it on a towel and use a medium-warm iron to press it dry. Trim the block to 15½" x 15½", which includes seam allowances.

Full-sized STARTER BOUQUET stem pattern. Stems show placement only. A ¼" stem width is recommended.

Whirling Tulips

WHIRLING TULIPS variation by the author.
Full quilt shown on page 36.

MAIN DESIGN (with narrow circle border):
  Finished block, 17" x 17"

VARIATION (with multiple-circle border):
  Finished block, 24" x 24"

ulips were one of the most popular flowers used by the Iznik tile artists in their designs. The word "tulip" comes from the Turkish word "tulpend" or "turban," which does indeed look very much like a tulip. These beautiful flowers are native to Turkey, and large varieties were cultivated long before they were introduced to the European countries in the 16th century.

The author used the WHIRLING TULIP block variation in this wallhanging.

Construction option: You can make the smaller tulip in three pieces as the pattern shows, or you can cut and appliqué it as one piece, then embroider the petal divisions.

Fabrics and supplies
MAIN DESIGN
  Flowers: assorted scraps
  Bias stems: 36" bias tape ¼" wide
    (instructions, page 20)
  Light background: 15" x 15"
  Darker background: 19" x 19"
    (main design only)
  Circle border: 15" x 15"
  Circle trim (optional): 66" bias tape or
    strip, ³⁄₁₆"–¼" wide
  Fusible interfacing: 2 pieces
    15" x 15"
  Freezer paper: two pieces 15" x 15"

VARIATION
  Circles: twelve fabric squares 13" x 13"
    in assorted colors
  Darker background: 25" x 25"
    (variation only)
  Fusible interfacing: twelve squares
    13" x 13"

Main design assembly
PREPARATION
  Please read the General Instructions, beginning on page 10, before starting your project.
  1. To make a master copy, trace the whole pattern (pages 38–41) on the dull side of a 15" freezer-paper square. Turn the master copy over and lightly trace the reversed image on the 15" light background square. To make a template copy, trace all the flowers and leaves on the dull side of the other 15" freezer-paper square.

2. On the template copy, add the number-letter labels. Cut the templates and press them, shiny side down, on the backs of the appropriate fabrics.

3. Cut the fabric pieces, adding ³/₁₆" turn-under allowances by eye as you cut. Turn the edges that will not be covered by other pieces.

Block assembly

4. Make three large tulip units and eight small tulip units, as shown in Fig. 2–2. Appliqué the leaves to the 14" light background square, then add the stems, followed by the flowers.

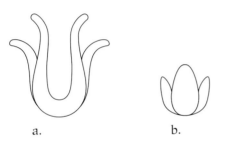

Fig. 2–2. Unit assembly. (a) Large tulip. (b) Small tulip.

5. Soak the block in warm water and remove the freezer paper. When the block is nearly dry, place it on a towel and use a medium-warm iron to press it dry.

Circles

6. Use the large-circle technique, on page 22, and the 15" fusible-interfacing square to turn the appliquéd square into a 12" circle. In the same manner, use the 15" squares of circle border fabric and interfacing to make a 13" circle.

7. Appliqué the 12" circle to the 13" border circle to complete the main design. Trim away the interfacings and circle border fabric from underneath the appliqué, leaving ¼" seam allowances.

8. If you are making the variation, skip to

the variation assembly. To finish the main design block, appliqué the 13" circle to the 19" darker background square. Trim the background from behind the circle as before. Appliqué a ¼" bias tape around the 13" circle, if desired. Press the block and trim it to 17½".

Variation assembly

9. After making the 13" main design circle, use the large-circle technique to make twelve 11" circles. With the main design centered on the 25" darker background square, slip four 11" circles underneath. Place a second round of four circles, then the last round (Fig. 2–3).

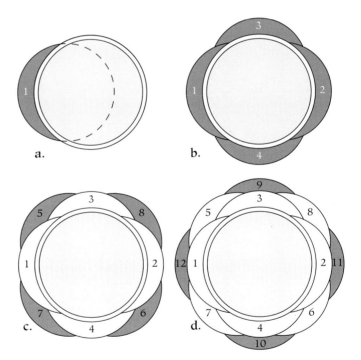

Fig. 2–3. Variation assembly: (a) Circle 1. (b) Round 1. (c) Round 2. (d) Round 3.

10. Press the circles to the background. Appliqué the edges that are visible. Cut away the background fabrics and interfacings from behind the circles. Press the block and trim it to 24½".

*W*hirling *T*ulips

Stems show placement only. A ³⁄₁₆"–¼" stem width is recommended.

circle border

1L
1A
1
1R
1B

2B
2
3R
2A
2
2C
2

1L
1R
1
1A
1B

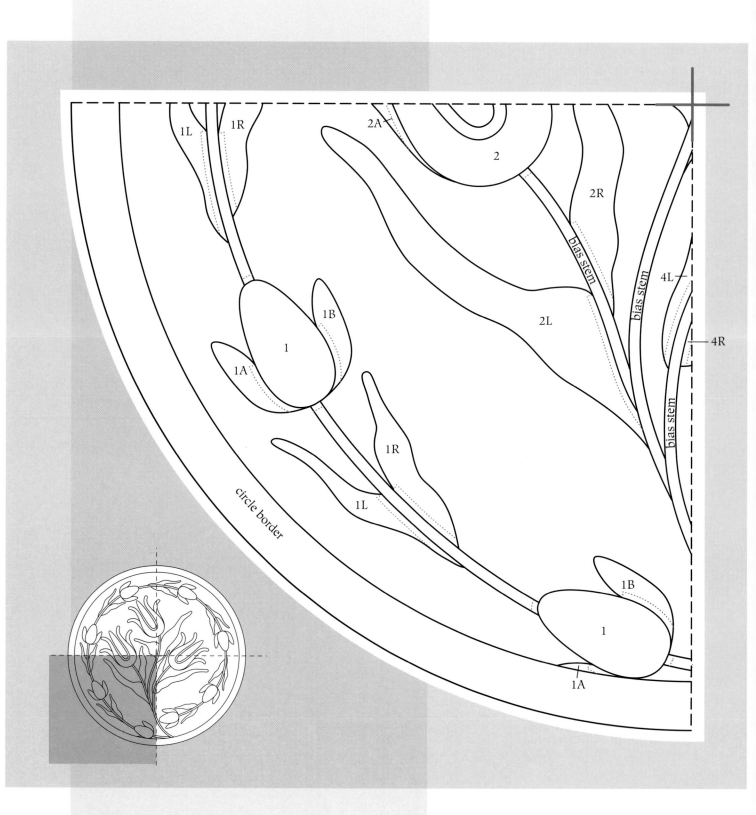

1L 1R 2A 2
  2R
1B bias stem
1 2L 4L
1A bias stem 4R
  bias stem
1R
circle border
1L
  1B
  1
  1A

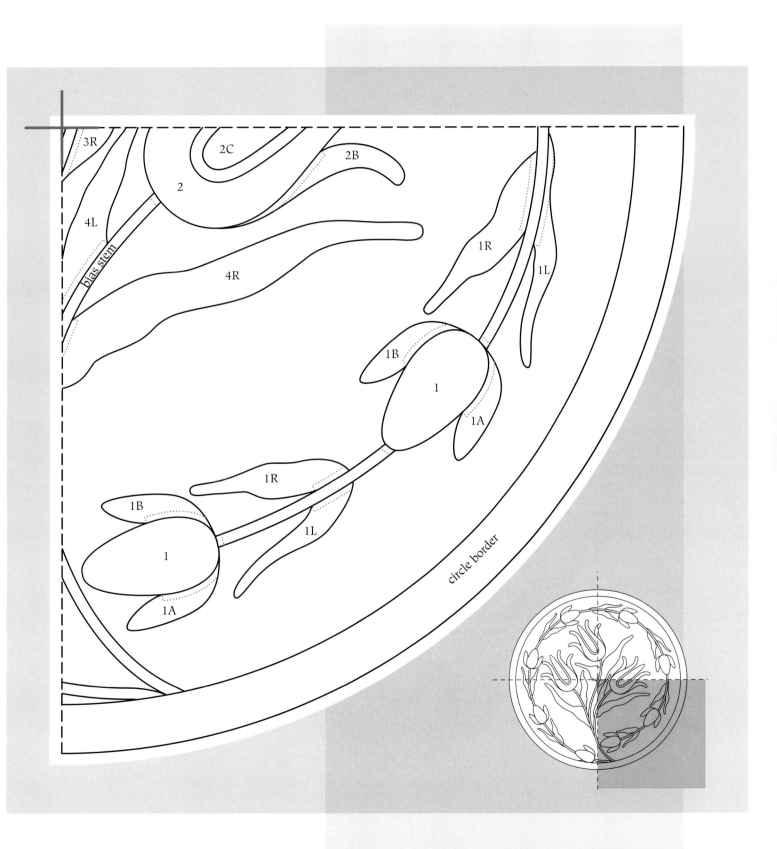

Carnations

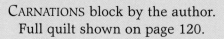

CARNATIONS block by the author.
Full quilt shown on page 120.

ome of the oldest embroideries on display in the Topkapi Palace museum in Istanbul were made by harem women to provide dowries for their daughters. Many of the designs include tulips, roses, pomegranates, and carnations. The inspiration to appliqué carnations came quite easily for me. The palace walls, tapestries, windows, pottery, and clothing were all gracefully adorned with this flower.

Finished block: 22" x 22"

Fabrics and supplies

Flowers and flowerpot: assorted scraps
Stems and leaves: assorted light, medium, and dark scraps
Background: 24" x 24"
Freezer paper: two squares 20" x 20"

Preparation

Please read the General Instructions, beginning on page 10, before starting your project.

1. Trace the whole pattern (pages 44–47) on the dull side of each 20" freezer-paper square. One is the master copy. The other is the template copy. Turn the master copy over and lightly trace the reversed image on the 24" background square.

2. On the template copy, add the number-letter labels. Cut the templates apart and press them, shiny side down, on the backs of the appropriate fabrics.

3. Cut the fabric pieces, adding a ³⁄₁₆" turn-under allowance by eye as you cut. Turn the edges that will not be covered by other pieces.

Block assembly

4. Appliqué the carnations, pink flowers, and stems in units, as shown in the Fig. 2–4 examples. Appliqué the stem units to the flower units.

5. Appliqué the flowerpot as a unit by using the steps shown in Fig. 2–5.

6. Appliqué all the petals separately to the background. Then add the flower units. Appliqué the flowerpot unit over the flower stems. Cut the background fabric from behind the appliqué, leaving a ¼" seam allowance.

Finishing

7. Soak the block in warm water and remove the freezer paper. When the block is nearly dry, press it dry on a towel. Trim the block to 22½" x 22½".

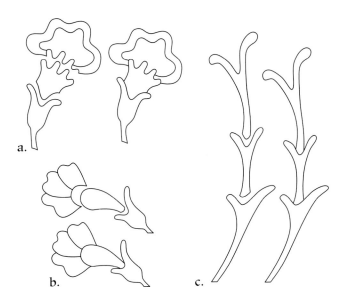

Fig. 2–4. Unit assembly: (a) Carnation. (b) Pink flower. (c) Stem.

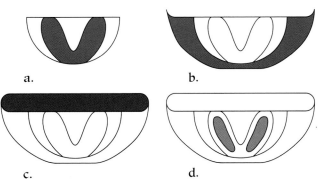

Fig. 2–5. Flowerpot unit.

Carnations

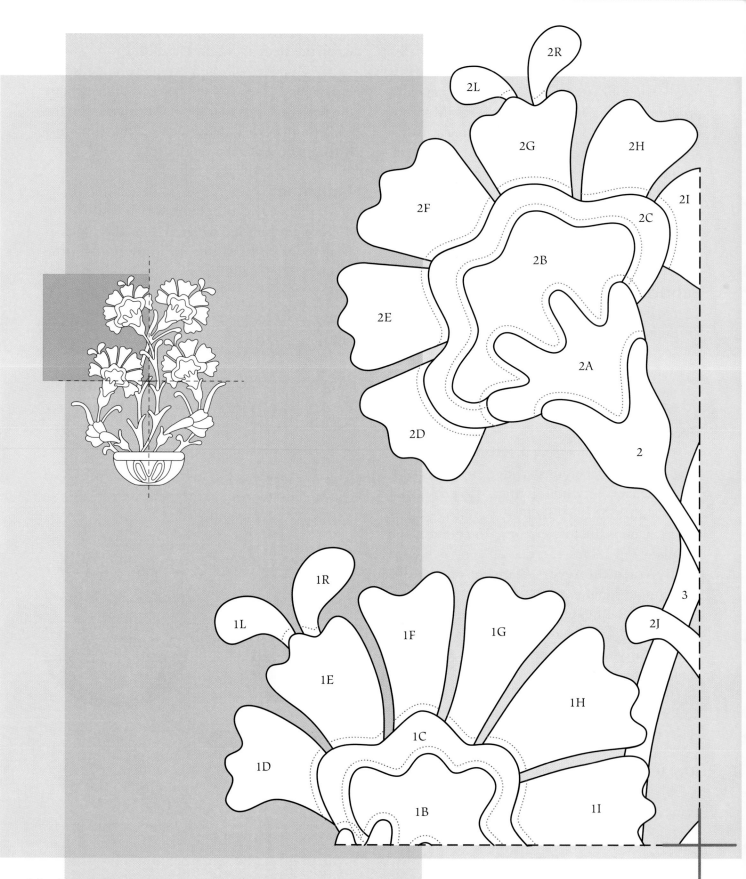

44 – Turkish Delights to Appliqué – Linda M. Poole

Carnations

1A
1B
1C
1I
3
1J
3J
1
1L
1R
3K
5E
5D
5C
5B
5A
2L
1K
7
7A
7B
7C
7L

Fancy Tulips

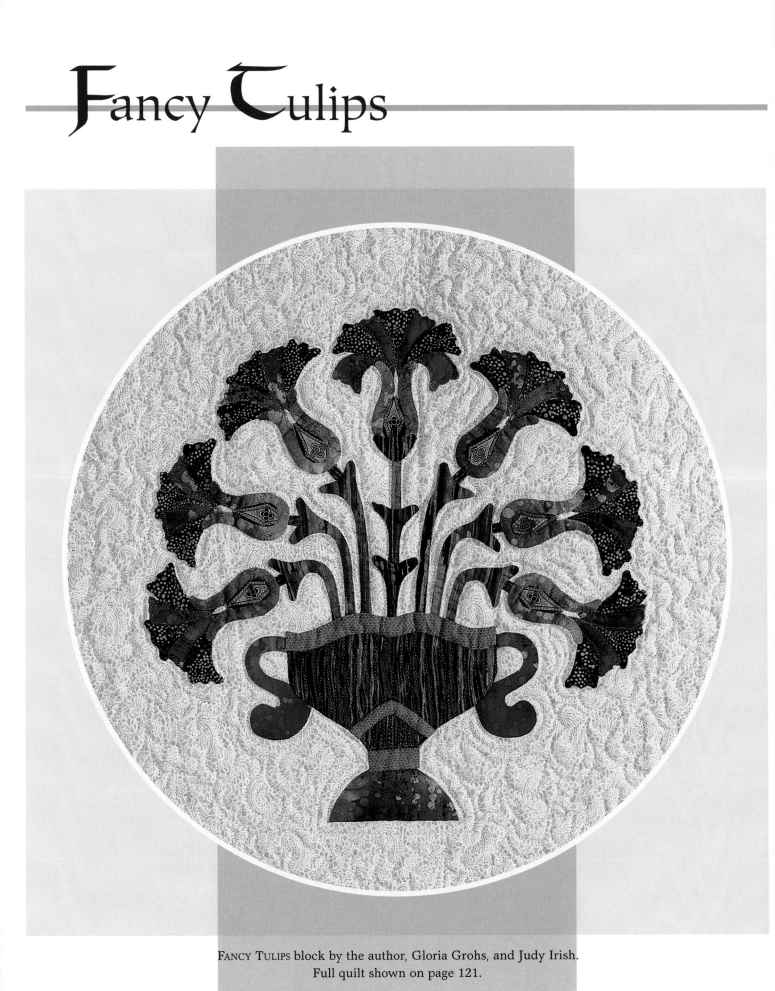

FANCY TULIPS block by the author, Gloria Grohs, and Judy Irish.
Full quilt shown on page 121.

o many tiles, so little time to quilt them all, but I was determined to appliqué one particular tile I had spotted in a mosque. The carnations in it formed a circular pattern, which piqued my curiosity. I wanted to learn how to set a pattern in a large circle. The result was FANCY TULIPS.

Finished block, 22½" x 22½"

Fabrics and Supplies

Stems and leaves: assorted light, medium, and dark scraps

Flowers and flowerpot: assorted scraps

Bias stems: 5" bias tape ³⁄₁₆"–¼" wide (instructions, page 20)

Light background: 22" x 22"

Darker background: 25" x 25"

Fusible interfacing: 22" x 22"

Circle trim (optional): 66" bias tape, ¼" wide

Freezer paper: two pieces 15" x 15"

Preparation

Please read the General Instructions, beginning on page 10, before starting your project.

1. Trace the pattern (pages 50–53) on the dull side of each 15" freezer-paper square. One is the master copy. The other is the template copy. Turn the master copy over and lightly trace the reversed image on the light background fabric square.

2. On the template copy, add the number-letter labels. Cut the templates apart and press them, shiny side down, on the backs of the appropriate fabrics.

3. Cut the fabric pieces, adding ³⁄₁₆" turn-under allowances by eye as you cut. Turn the edges that will not be covered by other pieces.

Block assembly

4. Make one center-tulip unit, six side-tulip units, one center-stem unit, and one flowerpot unit, as shown in Fig. 2–6.

5. Appliqué the pieces to the light background, starting with the stems and handles. Then add the tulip units. Appliqué the flowerpot over the edges of the stems and handles.

Finishing

6. Soak the block in warm water and remove the freezer paper. When the block is nearly dry, press it dry on a towel.

7. Use the large-circle technique, on page 22, and the 22" fusible-interfacing square to turn the appliquéd square into a 20" circle. Appliqué the circle to the 25" darker background square.

8. Appliqué the bias strip over the circle's edge, if desired. Trim the block to 23" x 23".

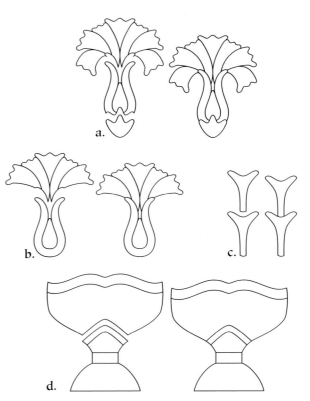

Fig. 2–6. Unit assembly: (a) Center tulip. (b) Side tulip. (c) Center stem. (d) Flowerpot.

Fancy Tulips

Stems show placement only. A ³⁄₁₆"–¼" stem width is recommended.

1G
1H
1I
1J
1C
1
1A
bias stem
6
7
2B
2C
2D
2E
2F
2
2A
bias stem
8
9
bias stem
10
2B
2C
2D
2E
2F
2A
2

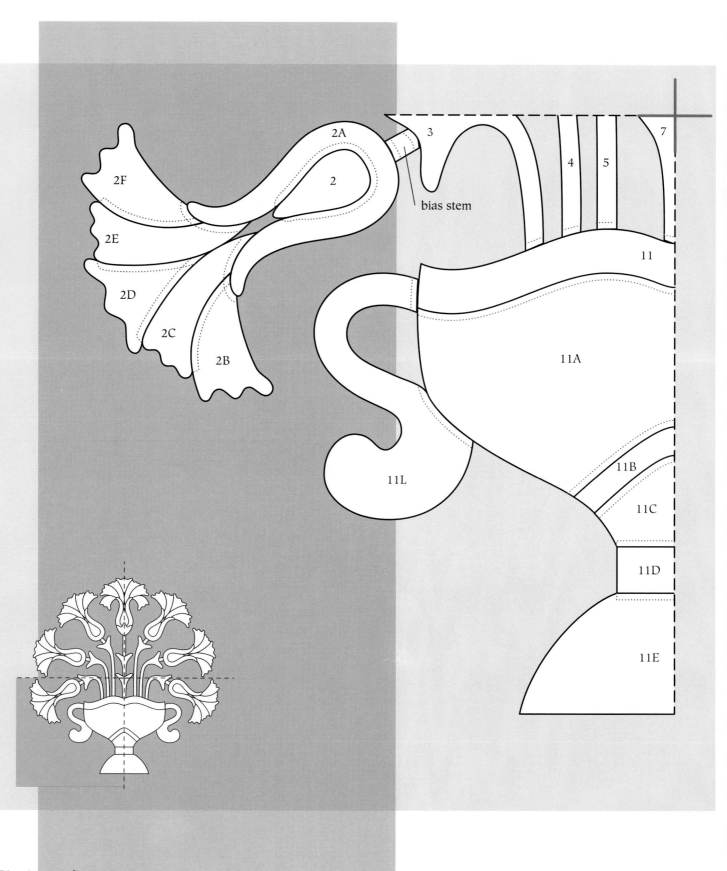

2A

2

2F

2E

2D

2C

2B

3

bias stem

4

5

7

11

11A

11L

11B

11C

11D

11E

7

8 9

10

2A

2

bias stem

2B

2C

2D

2E

2F

11

11A

11B

11C

11D

11E

11R

Glorious Bouquet

GLORIOUS BOUQUET block by Gloria Grohs.
Full quilt shown on page 121.

All the tiled floral bouquets that entranced my mind seemed to have a radiant glow to them, much like my mother's smile when she proudly shows me an appliqué piece she has sewn. In honor of my mom, Gloria, and the love I have for her, I fondly call this pattern GLORIOUS BOUQUET.

Finished block: 23" x 32"

Fabrics and Supplies

Flowers and flowerpot: assorted scraps
Stems and leaves: assorted light, medium and dark scraps
Light background: 17" x 24"
Darker background: 25" x 34"
Oval trim (optional): 65" bias tape, ¼" wide
Fusible interfacing: 17" x 24"
Freezer paper: two pieces 17" x 24"

Preparation

Please read the General Instructions, beginning on page 10, before starting your project.

1. Trace the pattern (pages 56–59) on the dull side of each 17" x 24" freezer-paper piece. One is the master copy. The other is the template copy. Trace the master copy on the 17" x 24" light background rectangle.

2. On the template copy, add the number-letter labels. Cut the template pieces apart and press them, shiny side down, on the backs of the appropriate fabrics.

3. Cut the fabric pieces, adding a ³⁄₁₆" turn-under allowance by eye as you cut. Turn the edges that will not be covered by other pieces.

Block assembly

4. Appliqué the various flower units and the stem-ring unit, as shown by the examples in Fig. 2–7.

5. Appliqué leaves 1L and 1R to the 17" x 24" light background, then add flower units 1 through 3. Attach the stem-ring unit, then flower units 4 through 7. Appliqué the flowerpot over the ends of the stems.

Finishing

6. Soak the block in warm water and remove the freezer paper. When the block is nearly dry, place it on a towel and use a medium-warm iron to press it dry.

7. Use the large-oval technique, on page 23, and the 17" x 24" fusible interfacing piece to turn the appliqué block into an oval. (For your oval "ruler," A–C is 11½" and B–C is 6½".)

8. Appliqué the edge of the finished oval to the 25" x 34" darker background rectangle. Trim the background fabric and the interfacing from behind the appliqué. Trim the piece to 23½" x 32½". Appliqué a ¼" bias tape or strip around the oval, if desired.

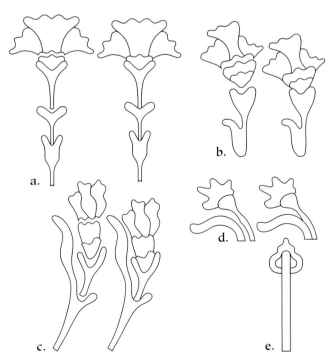

Fig. 2–7. Unit assembly: (a) Flower 1. (b) Flowers 2 and 3. (c) Flowers 4 and 5. (d) Flowers 6 and 7. (e) Stem-ring unit.

Glorious Bouquet

1

1A

1C

1D

1L

1E

2

2B

2A

2C

2D

2E

1F

4B

4

4A

4C

4F

4D

8

9

4E

1

1B

1C

1D

1R

1E

3A

3

3C

3B

3D

3E

1F

5A

5

5B

5C

5F

8

5D

9

5E

The labels within the pattern diagram read: 5E, 9, 5F, bias stem, 7, 7A, 7B, 10

Dancin' in the Moonlight

DANCIN' IN THE MOONLIGHT block by the author.
Full quilt shown on page 66.

ad and I went on a day-cruise from a port on the European side of Istanbul. The passenger ferry zigzagged lazily past villas, marble palaces, and stone fortresses along the Bosphorus Sea as we headed to our destination, the Prince Islands. Our ferry returned in the evening to the Asian side of Istanbul. I remember looking at the water splashing and dancing in the moonlight as our wonderful fairy tale day ended. What a beautiful combination: the flowers, the sea, and a very special day with Dad.

Finished block: 17" x 17"

Fabrics and Supplies

Flowers: assorted scraps
Stems and leaves: assorted light, medium, and dark scraps
Bias stems: 36" bias tape 3/16" wide (instructions, page 20)
Section A: 8" x 8"
Section B: 10" x 10"
Section C: 14" x 14"
Section D: 14" x 14"
Circle border: 15" x 15"
Darker background: 19" x 19"
Fusible interfacing:
    one piece 8" x 8"
    one piece 10" x 10"
    two pieces 14" x 14"
    one piece 15" x 15"
Freezer paper: two pieces 14" x 14"
Rickrack (optional): 50"

Preparation

Please read the General Instructions, beginning on page 10, before starting your project.

1. To make a master copy, trace the whole pattern (pages 62–65) on the dull side of one of the 14" freezer-paper squares. To make templates, trace the flowers and stems on the other 14" freezer paper square.

2. On the template copy, add the number-letter labels. Cut the template pieces apart and press them, shiny side down, on the backs of the appropriate fabrics.

3. Cut the fabric pieces, adding a 3/16" turn-under allowance by eye as you cut. Turn the edges under that will not be covered by other pieces.

Block assembly

POMEGRANATE FLOWER

4. Make the pomegranate flower unit (flower 2), as shown in Fig. 2–8. For a different look, omit pieces 2B through 2F (Fig. 2–9).

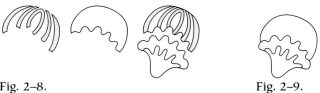

Fig. 2–8.   Fig. 2–9.

Fig. 2–8. Pomegranate flower unit.
Fig. 2–9. Omit 2B through 2F for a simpler flower.

OTHER FLOWER UNITS

5. Flowers 4 and 5 can also be pre-assembled in units before being appliquéd to the background. Make these units as shown in Fig. 2–10.

a.   b.

Fig. 2–10. Unit assembly. (a) Flower 4, (b) Flower 5.

continued on page 66

circle border

D

C

2B   2G   2C   2G

2A

B   2

A

1E

1D   B

1C   1R   2L

bias stem   2R

1   bias stem

C   1B

1A   B

Stems show placement only. A ³⁄₁₆" stem width is recommended.

circle border

2B
2G
2C
2G
2D
2G
2G
2E 2G
2A
2F
2
C
D
B
3A
3B
3C
3D
3E
3
D
2R
bias stem
4B 4B

C

D

B

1F

1L

bias stem

1R

bias stem

2H

5

5A

B

6E

B

C

C

circle border

6B

6D

6A

6

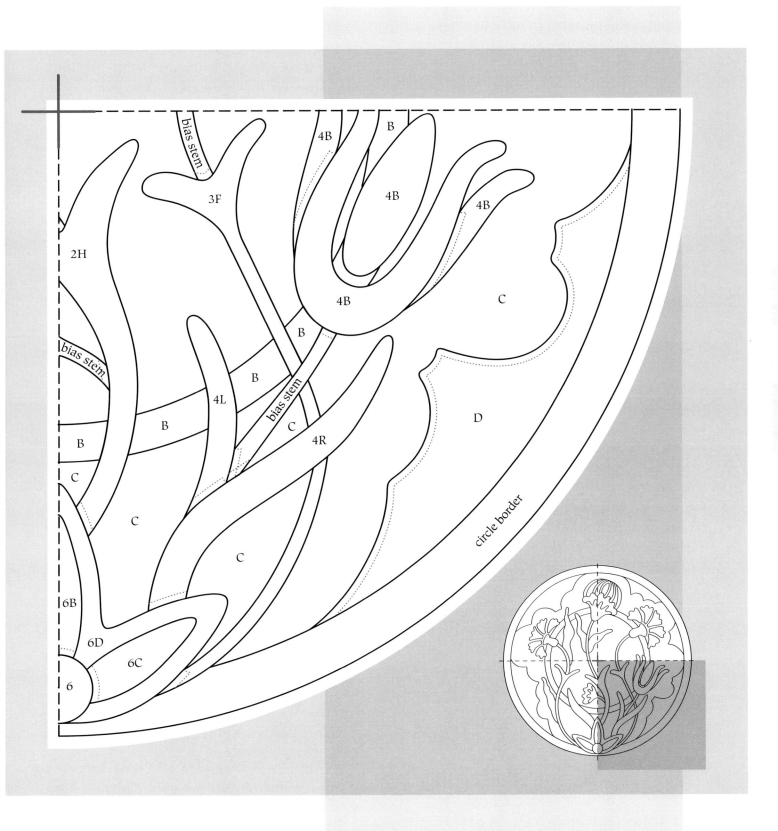

bias stem

4B

B

3F

4B

2H

4B

4B

C

B

bias stem

B

B

D

4L

bias stem

B

C

B

4R

C

C

circle border

C

6B

6D

6C

6

MEDALLION FLOWER

6. Appliqué petals 6A, 6B, and 6C to circle 6, then add this unit to piece 6D (Fig. 2–11).

Fig. 2–11. Medallion flower unit.

BACKGROUND UNIT

7. Refer to the large-circle technique on page 22. Using the circle fabric squares and the fusible interfacing squares of the same size, make circles for sections A (6½"), B (7½"), and D (12"), and the circle border (13").

8. Similar to the large-circle technique, trace the outline of section C on a 14" fusible-interfacing square. Sew the section C fabric square and the interfacing square, right sides together, on the traced line. Trim away the excess fabric, clip seam allowances as needed, and turn the section right side out.

9. Appliqué section C to section D. Appliqué circle A to circle B. Trim away the fabrics and interfacings from underneath the top layers of both units, leaving ¼" seam allowances. Center and appliqué the A/B unit to the C/D unit. Trim as before.

10. Turn the master copy over. Center the background unit on the master copy and lightly trace the reversed images of flowers 1 through 6 with their leaves and stems.

Fig. 2–12. Appliqué section C to section D.

APPLIQUÉ

11. To appliqué the flowers to the background unit, gently peel back some of the freezer paper as needed to remove bulk. Appliqué the leaves for flowers 1 and 2 first. Add flower 5, then add the petals for flowers 1 and 3.

12. Appliqué the bias stems for flowers 1 through 3. Next, finish flowers 1 through 3 with their stems 1F, 2H, and 3F. Add leaf 6E, the bias stem for flower 4, and flower 4 with its leaves. Finish with the medallion flower unit.

13. Center the appliquéd circle on the 19" darker background square and pin. Lightly glue rickrack under the edge of the appliquéd flower circle and pin. Appliqué the circle and tack stitch the rickrack to hold it in place. Trim away the background from under the appliqué.

Finishing

14. If there is any remaining freezer paper, soak the block in warm water and remove the paper. When the block is nearly dry, place it on a towel and use a medium-warm iron to press it dry. Trim the block to 17½" x 17½".

DANCIN' IN THE MOONLIGHT quilt, 33" x 28". Hand appliquéd and embellished by the author; machine quilted by Judy Irish, Arlington, Washington.

Sophia

SOPHIA block by Judy Brumbaugh.
Full wallhanging shown on page 68.

Sophia

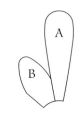

The Hagia Sophia, in Istanbul, was once known as Megalo Ecclesia, which means "colossal church." It was first built early in the fourth century. It burned twice, and the present structure, which tourists can visit, was rebuilt in 532. It is a true treasure and one of the most outstanding monuments ever built. It is called Hagia Sophia because it was dedicated to the Holy Wisdom, and Sophia means wisdom.

Finished block: 15" x 15"

Fabrics and Supplies

Center flower: assorted scraps
Outer flowers: 6 light-colored pieces, 5" x 5"
Light background: 15" x 15"
Darker background: 17" x 17"
Bias-tape design: 6½ yards bias tape ³⁄₁₆" wide (instructions, page 20)
Freezer paper:
    15" x 15"
    12" x 12"

The author used the SOPHIA block variation in this wallhanging.

Preparation

Please read the General Instructions, beginning on page 10, before starting your project.

1. Trace the pattern (pages 70–73) on the dull side of the 15" freezer-paper square to make a master copy. Lightly retrace the master copy on the 15" light background square.

Center flower

2. To make appliqué templates, trace the center flower pattern on the 12" freezer-paper square. Add the letter labels to the templates.

3. Cut the templates apart and press them, shiny side down, on the backs of the appropriate fabrics.

4. Cut the fabric petals, adding a ³⁄₁₆" turn-under allowance by eye as you cut. Turn the edges that will not be covered by other petals.

5. Appliqué petal A to petal B (Fig. 2–13). Make a total of six A/B units. Appliqué the units to one another in a circle (Fig. 2–14). Appliqué the center circle C on top of the A/B units (Fig. 2–15).

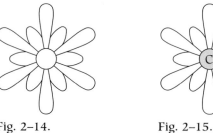

Fig. 2–13. Make A/B units.

Fig. 2–14.   **Fig. 2–15.**

Fig. 2–14. Join the A/B units in a circle.
Fig. 2–15. Appliqué piece C in the middle.

Inner bias-tape design

6. On each 5" fabric square, trace the inner bias-tape design, as shown in Fig. 2–16. Glue, pin, or press down bias loop 1. Appliqué the inside edge only. Working loop by loop, appliqué the other four loops in the same way (Fig. 2–17). Repeat for the other five 5" squares.

7. With small scissors, trim away the 5" squares a scant ¹⁄₁₆" inside the outer edge of the bias tape around each flower (Fig. 2–18).

8. Place all the bias-tape units on the 15" light background square and appliqué the outside edges of the inner bias-tape design. Position and appliqué the center-flower unit.

Outer bias-tape design

9. Glue, pin, or press down the outer bias-tape design on the light background square. As before, appliqué only the inside edges of the design. Then trim away the square a scant ¹⁄₁₆" inside the outer edge of the bias tape

10. Appliqué the whole design to the 17" darker background square. Trim the background from behind the appliqué, leaving a ¼" seam allowance.

Finishing

11. Soak the block in warm water and remove the freezer paper. When the block is nearly dry, place it on a towel and use a medium-warm iron to press it dry. Trim the block to 15½" x 15½".

Inspiration for SOPHIA.

Fig. 2–16. Trace the inner bias-tape design on the 5" squares.

Fig. 2–17. Appliqué the inside of each loop.

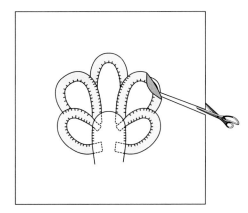

Fig. 2–18. Trim the square under the bias-tape loops.

Stems show placement only. A ³⁄₁₆" stem width is recommended.

bias tape

bias tape

bias tape

A

B

A

C

B

C

B

B

A

A

bias tape

bias tape

bias tape

Spring Green Wreath

SPRING GREEN WREATH block by the author.
Full wallhanging shown on page 75.

My hotel in Istanbul was located in the historical section of Taksim Square. As I walked to explore this wondrous city, I noticed not only with my eyes, but also with my sense of smell, the beautiful bouquets of tulips and roses in the market. In whatever direction I turned, flowers were in abundance. I happily purchased flowers several times. SPRING GREEN WREATH is my tribute to this eternal springtime feeling I had walking the streets of Taksim Square.

Finished block: 16" x 16"

Fabrics and Supplies

Flowers: assorted scraps

Stems and leaves: assorted light, medium, and dark scraps

Bias stems: 36" bias tape ³⁄₁₆"–¼" wide (instructions, page 20)

Background: 18" x 18"

Freezer paper: two pieces 15" x 15"

Preparation

Please read the General Instructions, beginning on page 10, before starting your project.

1. Trace the pattern (pages 76–79) on the dull side of each 15" freezer-paper square. One is the master copy. The other is the template copy. Turn the master copy over and lightly trace the reversed image on the background square.

2. On the template copy, write the number-letter labels on the pattern pieces. Cut the templates apart and press them, shiny side down, on the backs of the appropriate fabrics.

3. Cut the fabric pieces, adding a ³⁄₁₆" turn-under allowance by eye as you cut. Turn the edges that will not be covered by other pieces.

Block assembly

4. Make four large flower units, four small flower units, and nine bud units, Fig. 2–19.

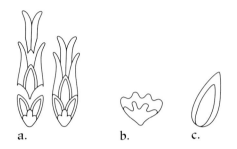

Fig. 2–19. Unit assembly: (a) Large flower. (b) Small flower. (c) Bud.

5. Determine which short stems will be appliquéd under longer stems. Appliqué the short stems to the 18" background square first, then the longer stems. Add the large bias-stem circle.

6. Appliqué the flowers and buds. Cut the background fabric from behind the appliqué.

Finishing

7. Soak the block in warm water and remove the freezer paper. When the block is nearly dry, place it on a towel and use a medium-warm iron to press it dry. Trim the block to 16½" x 16½".

The author used the SPRING GREEN WREATH block variation in this wallhanging.

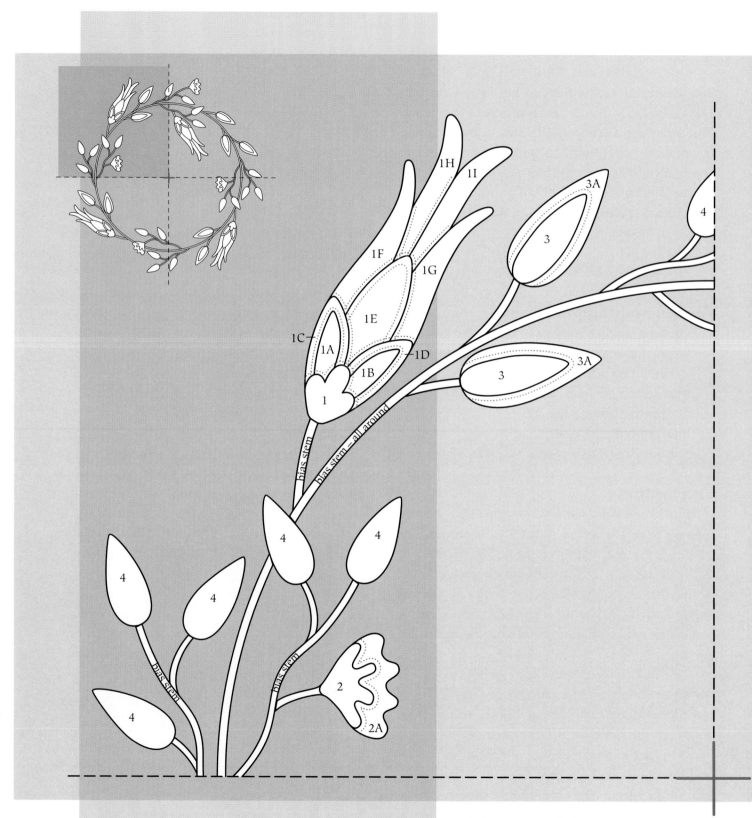

Stems show placement only. A ³⁄₁₆"–¼" stem width is recommended.

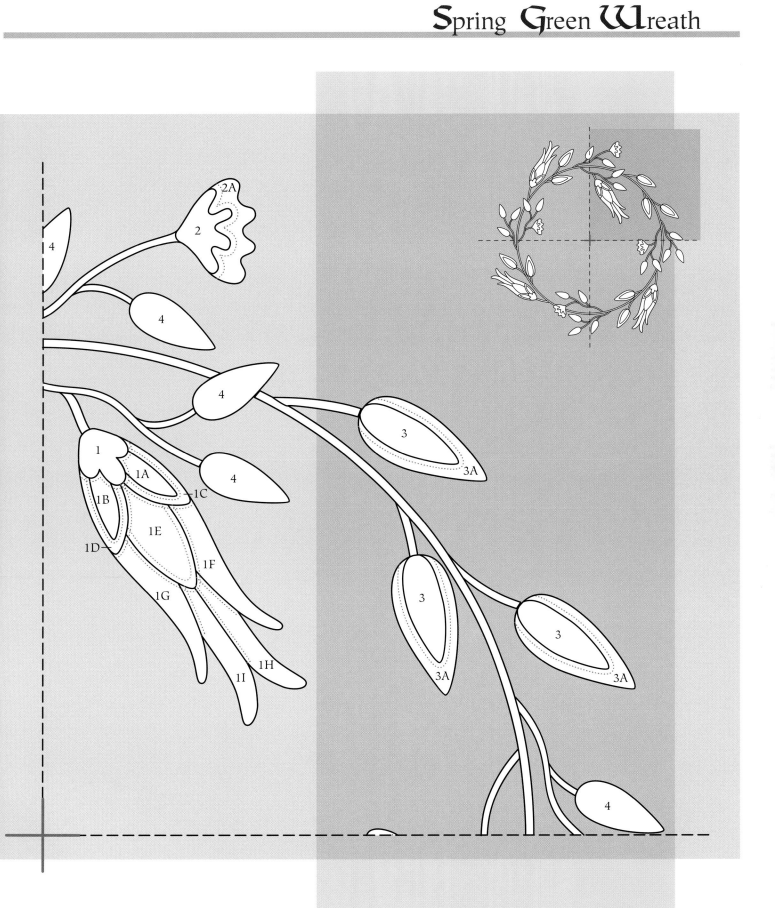

Spring Green Wreath

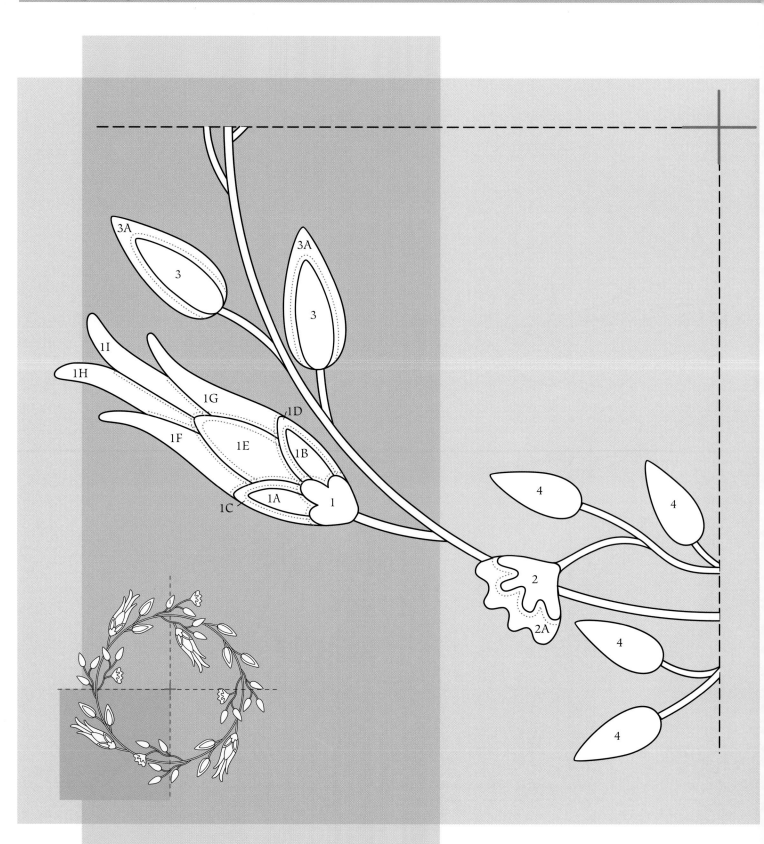

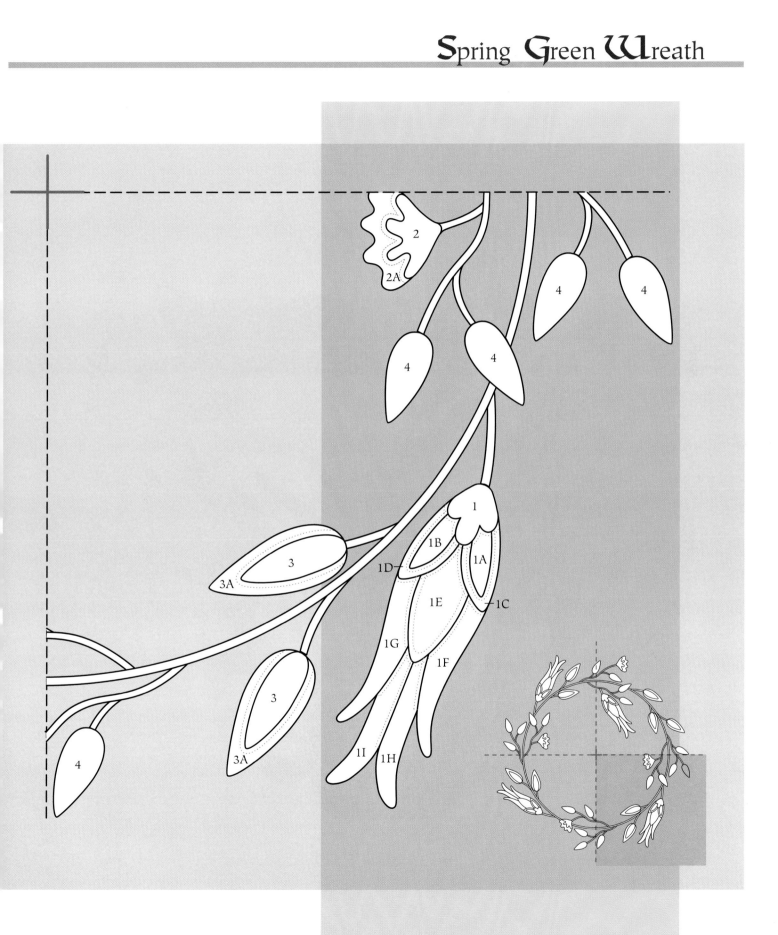

Sᴜɴ Dᴀɴᴄᴇ by the author.
Full quilt shown on page 31.

designed this pattern as a celebration piece to all the artisans who created the beautiful tiles, pottery, and illuminated manuscripts that give Turkey its rich culture in the arts. When I see the flowers, it seems as if they sway and shine their faces to the sun, thus the name SUN DANCE.

Finished block: 26" x 26"

Fabrics and Supplies

Flowers, buds, and flowerpot: assorted scraps

Stems and leaves: assorted light, medium, and dark scraps

Bias stems: 36" bias tape ³⁄₁₆"–¼" wide (instructions, page 20)

Light background: 23" x 23"

Darker background: 28" x 28"

Fusible interfacing: 23" x 23"

Freezer paper: two pieces 23" x 23"

Preparation

Please read the General Instructions, beginning on page 10, before starting your project.

1. Trace the pattern (pages 82–85) on the dull side of each 23" freezer-paper square. One is the master copy. The other is the template copy. Turn the master copy over and lightly trace the reversed image on the background square.

2. On the template copy, write the number-letter labels on the pattern pieces. Cut the templates apart and press them, shiny side down, on the backs of the appropriate fabrics.

3. Cut the fabric pieces, adding a ³⁄₁₆" turn-under allowance by eye as you cut. Turn the edges that will not be covered by other pieces.

Flowers, leaves, and pot

4. Make the flowers, buds, and flowerpot units as shown in Fig. 2–20.

Block assembly

5. Appliqué the leaves for flowers 1 and 3 to the light 23" background square. Add flowerpot handles 4L and 4R, then flowers 1 and 2, and leaves 2R and 2L.

6. Add the short bias stems for the buds, then their long stems, and finally the buds themselves. Appliqué the stems for both flower 3 units, then the flowers. Add the flowerpot over the edges of the stems and handles.

Finishing

7. Soak the block in warm water and remove the freezer paper. When the block is nearly dry, place it on a towel and use a medium-warm iron to press it dry.

8. Use the large-circle technique, on page 22, and the 23" fusible-interfacing square to turn the appliquéd block into a 21" circle. Appliqué the circle to the 28" darker background square. Trim the square to 26½".

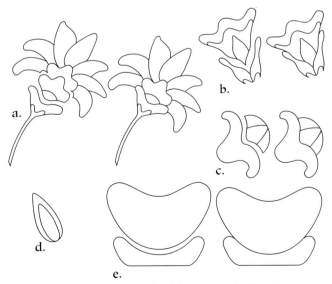

Fig. 2–20. Unit assembly. (a) Flower 1, (b) Flower 2, (c) Flower 3, (d) Bud, (e) Flowerpot.

1E

1D

1C

1B

1A

2D

1L

1

5A

5

1R

bias stem

5A

5

2L

5A

5

bias stem

Stems show placement only. A ³⁄₁₆"–¼" stem width is recommended.

3C

3B

3A

3

5A

5

bias stem

bias stem

2L

3R

bias stem

3L

4L

4

4A

2

2R

6A

6

6

6A

6A

6

1

bias stem

bias stem

bias stem

bias stem

bias stem

3A

3B

3C

3

4R

4

4A

Floral Festivities

FLORAL FESTIVITIES block by the author.
Full quilt shown on page 92.

alking among the meticulously planted flower beds on the grounds of different mosques and palaces, I found the purest form of delight and enchantment for my soul. Quietly sitting on a garden bench, I envisioned the days long past, when women gathered fresh flowers to add to their daily baths, to adorn their finely combed hair, and to fill colorfully painted vases until they overflowed with the wonderful aromas of the garden. The gardens bring such joy to any fortunate person who experiences them.

Finished block: 17" x 17"

Fabrics and Supplies

Flowers: assorted scraps
Stems and leaves: assorted light, medium, and dark scraps
Bias stems: 36" bias tape ³⁄₁₆" wide (instructions, page 20)
Light background: 14" x 14"
Circle border: 15" x 15"
Darker background: 19" x 19'
Fusible interfacing:
 14" x 14"
 15" x 15"
Freezer paper: two pieces 14" x 14"

Preparation

Please read the General Instructions, beginning on page 10, before starting your project.

1. Trace the whole pattern (pages 88–91) on the dull side of one 14" freezer-paper square. It is the master copy. Turn the master copy over and lightly trace the reversed image on the 14" light background square. On the dull side of the other 14" freezer-paper square, copy all the flowers and leaves. This is the template copy.

2. On the template copy, add the number-letter labels. Cut the templates apart and press them, shiny side down, on the backs of the appropriate fabrics.

3. Cut the fabric pieces, adding ³⁄₁₆" turn-under allowances by eye as you cut. Turn the edges that will not be covered by other pieces.

Block assembly

4. Make six flower units and one leaf unit, as shown in Figs. 2-21a-f, and Fig. 2-21g, on page 92.

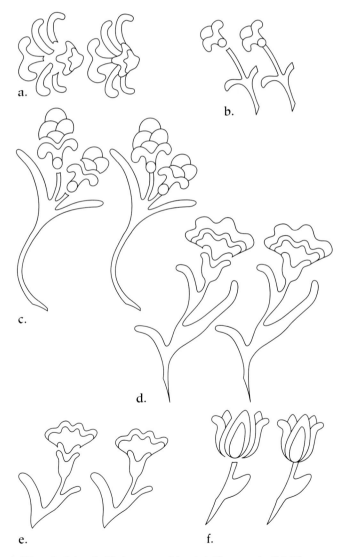

Fig. 2–21a–f. Unit assembly. (a) Flower 1, (b) Flower 2, (c) Flower 3, (d) Flower 4, (e) Flower 5, (f) Flower 6.

continued on page 92

circle border

2B

2A

2

1F

1E

1D

1A

1

1C

bias stem

1R

2C

3E

3C

3D

3B

3A

3

3C

3B

3A

3

3F

4

Stems show placement only. A ³⁄₁₆" stem width is recommended.

circle border

4C

4B

4A

4

3C

3B

3D

3A

5B

5A

5

6C 6A 6D

5

4

6C   6A   6D

6B   6E

6

10A

12

6F

10

circle border

8R

7R   9R

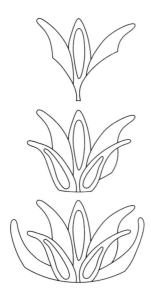

Fig. 2–21g. Leaves.

FLORAL FESTIVITIES, 24" x 24". Hand appliquéd, pieced, and embellished by the author. In each corner is a quarter-circle carefully laid over the 13" border appliquéd circle, letting the pale teal green peek from the background.

5. To appliqué the pieces and units to the 14" light background square, start with flower units 2 and 4. Then add flower units 5 and 6. Appliqué flower unit 3.

6. Add leaves 1L and 1R, then the bias stem for flower 1. Appliqué flower-unit 1 and the leaf unit to the background. Trim the background from underneath the appliqué, leaving a ¼" seam allowance.

Finishing

7. Soak the block in warm water and remove the freezer paper. When the block is nearly dry, place it on a towel and use a medium-warm iron to press it dry.

8. Use the large-circle technique, on page 22, and the 14" fusible-interfacing square to turn the appliquéd block into a 12" circle. Use the circle border square and the 15" fusible-interfacing square to make the 13" border circle.

9. Appliqué the 12" appliquéd circle on the 13" border circle. Trim the background and fusible interfacings from under the appliqué, leaving a ¼" seam allowance.

10. Appliqué the 13" circle to the 19" background square. Trim the background from underneath the circle. Press the block and trim it to 17½" x 17½".

Mediterranean Medallion

MEDITERRANEAN MEDALLION block by the author.
Full quilt shown on page 124.

Mediterranean Medallion

ach day, as I walked about Istanbul, enjoying the treasures and pleasures that Turkey had to offer, this particular medallion shape seemed be everywhere. It mysteriously called to me and piqued my curiosity about the Iznik tile art. This quilt design will always signify my quest for the heart and soul of this amazing country.

Finished block: 27" x 40"

Fabrics and Supplies

Flowers and decorative pieces: assorted scraps

Stems and leaves: assorted light, medium, and dark scraps

Section A: 20" x 24"

Section B: 20" x 24"

Section C: 24" x 30"

Darker background: 29" x 42"

Fusible interfacing:
two pieces 20" x 24"
one piece 24" x 30"

Bias stems: 36" bias tape ¼" wide (instructions page 20)

Freezer paper:
29" x 42"
20" x 24"

Background unit

Please read the General Instructions, beginning on page 10, before starting your project.

1. Trace the whole pattern (pages 96–103) on the dull side of the 29" x 42" piece of freezer-paper. This is the master copy. From the master copy, trace the outline of section C on the 24" x 30" piece of interfacing. Trace section B on one of the 20" x 24" interfacings, and section A on the other.

2. For sections A, B, and C, pair the fabric pieces, right sides together, with the interfacing pieces of the same size. Sew each pair on the traced line, trim away the excess fabric, clip seam allowances as needed for section C, and turn the sections right side out (similar to the large-circle technique on page 22).

3. Appliqué section A to section B (Fig. 2–22). Trim the excess fabric and interfacings from behind section A, leaving a ¼" seam allowance. In the same manner, sew the A/B unit to section C (Fig. 2–23). Trim as before.

Fig. 2–22. Appliqué section A to section B.

Fig. 2–23. Appliqué unit A/B to section C.

Block assembly

4. Trace the flower section on the 20" x 24" freezer paper. This is the template copy. Add the number-letter labels. Cut the pieces apart and press them, shiny side down, on the backs of the appropriate fabrics.

5. Cut the fabric pieces, adding a ³⁄₁₆" turn-under allowance by eye as you cut. Turn the edges that will not be covered by other pieces.

6. Make the flowers, flower holder, and finials (9 and 9A) in units, as shown in Fig. 2–24. For flowers 1 through 3, you can appliqué the little circles to each petal or embellish them with buttons, beads, or crystals.

7. Appliqué the bias stems for flowers 1 and 3 first, then the stems for flowers 4 and 7. Add their leaves and, finally, the flowers.

8. Appliqué the bias stems for tulips 5 and 6, slipping the stems through the stem ring (piece 11). Then add flowers 5 and 6.

9. Add the bias stem for flower 2 and then the flower itself. To complete the medallion unit, appliqué the stem ring and the decorative flower holder unit.

Finishing

10. Use the master copy to trace the whole medallion outline on the 29" x 42" dark background. Appliqué the entire medallion unit to the darker background, leaving the top and bottom open to slip in finial pieces 9 and 9A. Add 9 and 9A and appliqué the openings. Trim the background fabric from behind the appliqué, leaving a ¼" seam allowance.

11. Soak the piece in warm water and remove the freezer paper. When the piece is nearly dry, place it on a towel and use a medium-warm iron to press it dry. Trim it to 27½" x 40½".

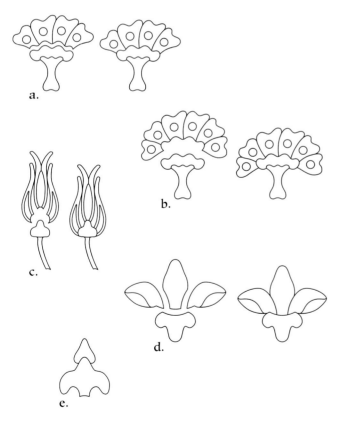

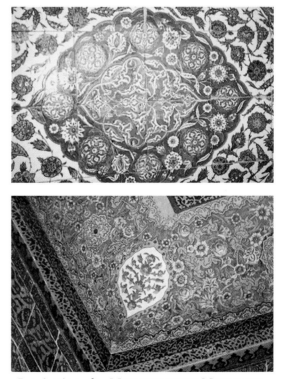

Fig. 2–24. Unit assembly: (a) Flowers 1 and 3. (b) Flower 2. (c) Flowers 4 through 7 (d) Decorative flower holder. (e) Finial.

Inspirations for MEDITERRANEAN MEDALLION.

BACKGROUND UNIT (half pattern, pages 96–99)

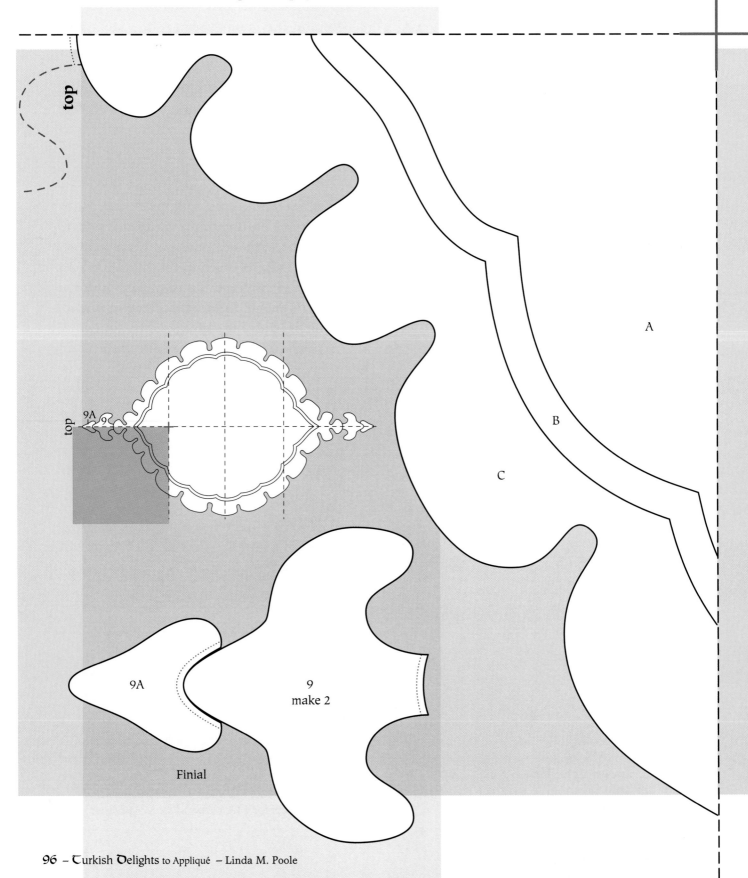

top

9A 9

top

A

B

C

9A

9
make 2

Finial

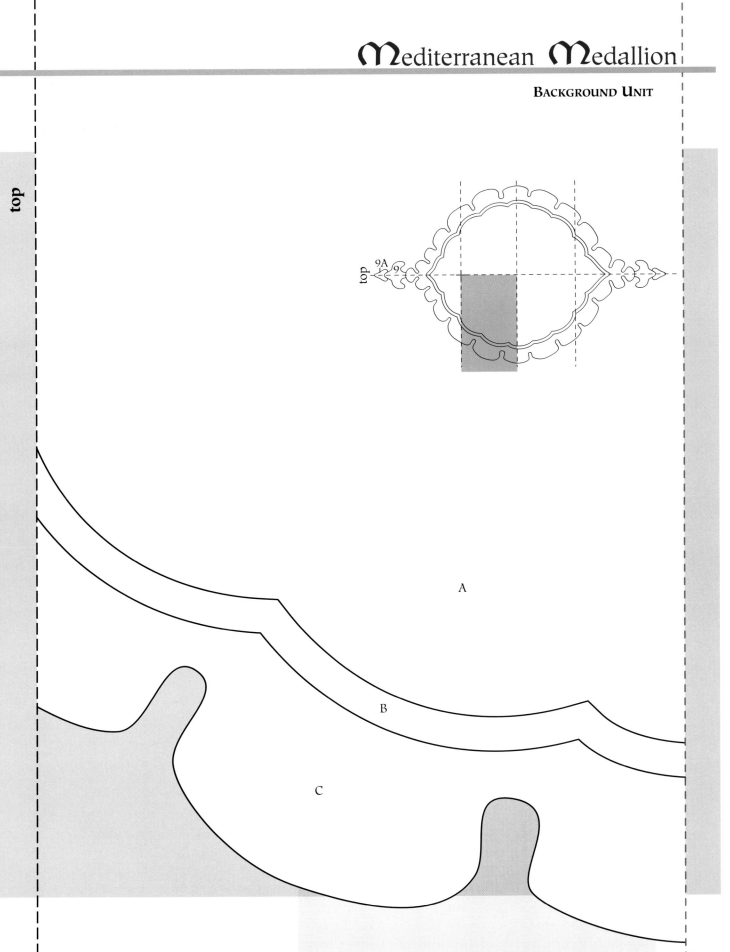

top

9A
9
top

A

B

C

BACKGROUND UNIT

top

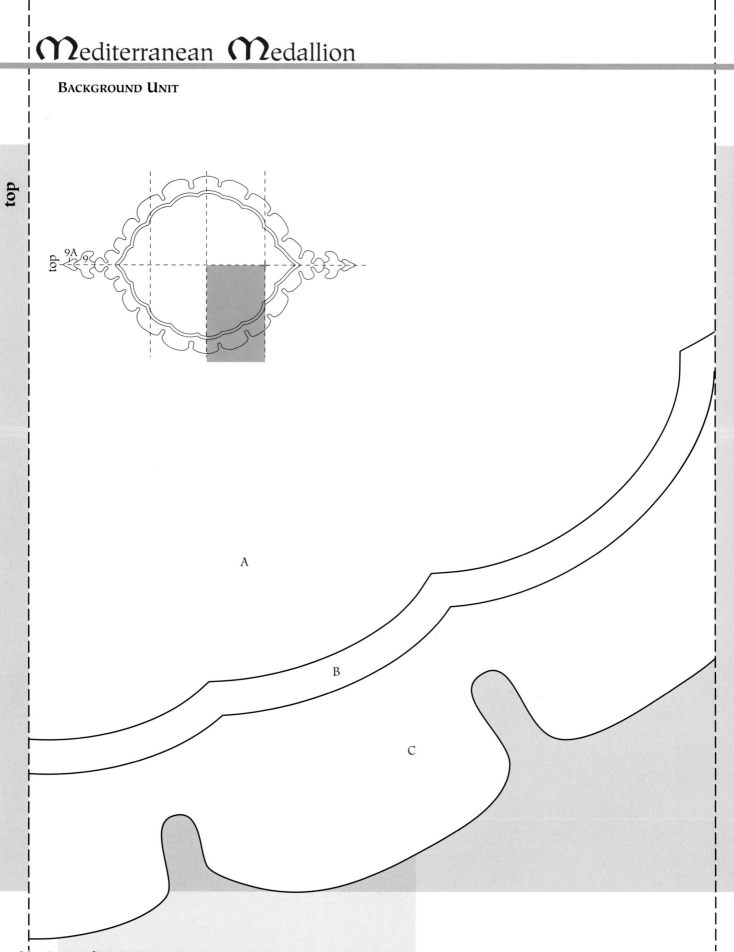

top

9A   9

A

B

C

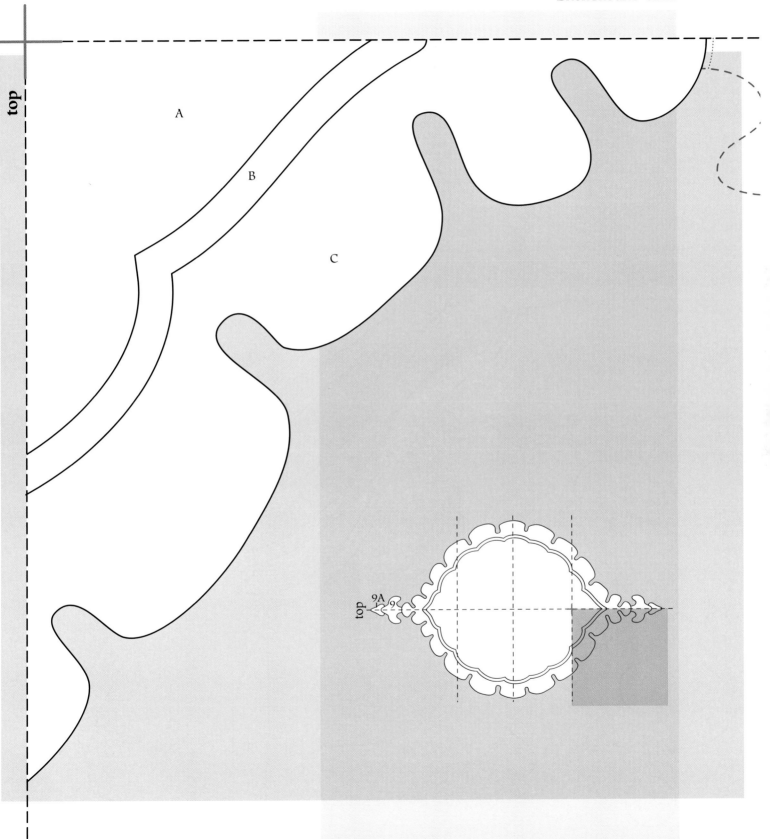

FLOWER APPLIQUÉ

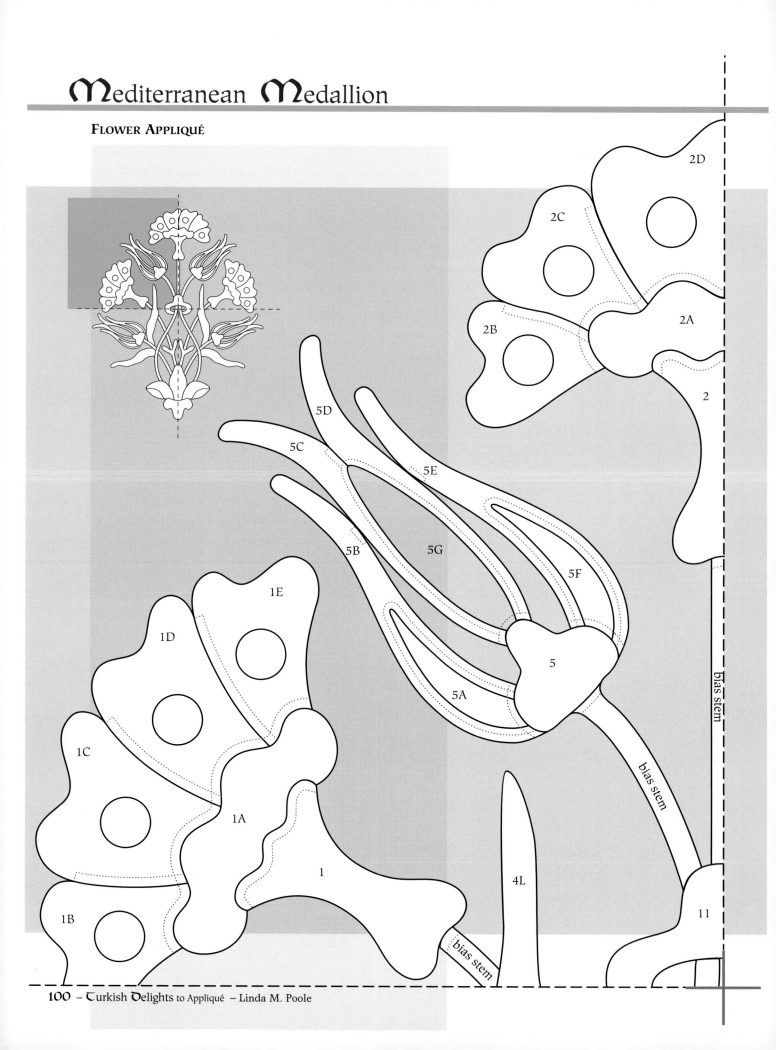

FLOWER APPLIQUÉ

FLOWER APPLIQUÉ

1B

4D
4E
4C
4F
4B
4G
4A
4

4L
bias stem
bias stem
bias stem
1F
11

4R

8
8A
8B
11

11

3E

FLOWER APPLIQUÉ

bias stem

7L

7B

7C

7A

7D

7G

7E

7

6F

7F

7R

bias stem

bias stem

8

8C

8D

11

Cat's Eye

CAT'S EYE block by the author.
Full quilt, with cat's eyes, shown on page 31.

he cutest little kitty cat followed me around the courtyard of the Topkapi Palace one day. This kitty was quite young, and he enjoyed hiding among the bushes and trees. Every so often, he would show himself to me in quite an impish little way. I thought back to the days when the palace was full of activity. Perhaps the children had delighted in playing with these little creatures. I named this little guy "Palace Cat, Keeper of the Tiles," and he was the perfect inspiration for all the cats' eyes I appliquéd in this quilt (page 31).

Finished block: 22" x 22"

Fabrics and Supplies

Tulips and decorative pieces:
    assorted scraps
Stems and leaves: assorted light, medium, and dark scraps
Section A: 14" x 14"
Section B: 14" x 14"
Section C: 14" x 14"
Section D: 14" x 14"
Circle border: 15" x 15"
Background: 24" x 24"
Fusible interfacing:
    four pieces 14" x 14"
    one piece 15" x 15"
Freezer paper: two pieces 14" x 14"

Palace cat.

Preparation

Please read the General Instructions, beginning on page 10, before starting your project.

1. To make a master copy, trace the whole pattern (pages 106–109) on one of the 14" freezer-paper squares.

2. To make templates for the tulips, piece 1G, and the decorative pieces, trace them on the other 14" freezer-paper square. Add the number-letter labels. Cut the templates apart and press them, shiny side down, on the backs of the appropriate fabrics.

3. Cut the fabric pieces, adding a 3/16" turn-under allowance by eye as you cut. Turn the edges that will not be covered by other pieces.

continued on page 110

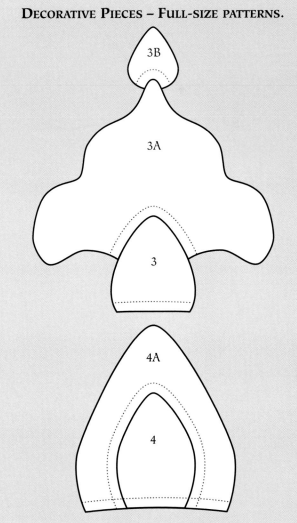

DECORATIVE PIECES – FULL-SIZE PATTERNS.

Cat's Eye

circle border

D

C

B

A

1F

1D

1B

1E

1

1G

2C

2D

2E

2B

Cat's Eye

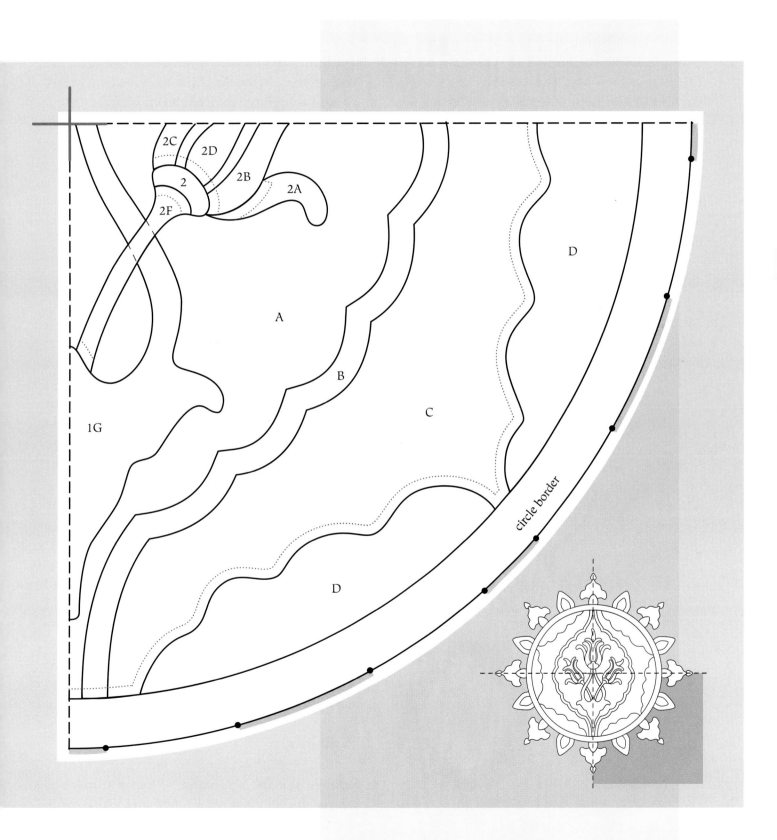

2C
2D
2B
2
2A
2F
A
B
C
D
1G
D
circle border

Background unit

4. Refer to the large-circle technique on page 22. Using the section D and circle border fabric squares and the fusible interfacing squares of the same size, make circles for section D (12") and the circle border (13").

5. Trace the outline of section A on a 14" interfacing square. Repeat for sections B and C. Pair the interfacing squares with the section fabric squares. Sew each pair together on the traced line. Proceed as you would for making large circles, clipping seam allowances as needed.

6. Appliqué section A to section B (Fig. 2–25). Trim the fabric and interfacings from behind A, leaving a ¼" seam allowance. Appliqué section C to section D and trim as before (Fig. 2–26). Appliqué unit A/B to unit C/D and trim again (Fig. 2–27).

Fig. 2–25. Appliqué section A to section B.

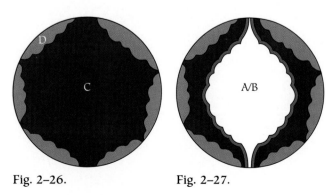

Fig. 2–26.   Fig. 2–27.

Fig. 2–26. Appliqué section C to section D.
Fig. 2–27. Appliqué unit A/B to unit C/D.

Block assembly

7. The tulips and decorative pieces can be appliquéd as units before being sewn to the background. Make the three tulip units and eight of each decorative unit, as shown in Fig. 2–28.

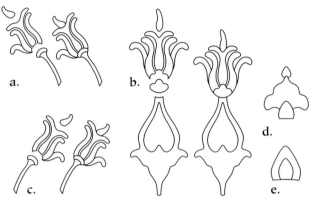

Fig. 2-28. Unit assembly: (a) Left tulip, (b) Center tulip, (c) Right tulip, (d) Decorative piece 1, (e) Decorative piece 2.

8. Use the master pattern to lightly trace the tulips and decorative pieces on the background unit. Appliqué the left tulip unit to the background first. Add piece 1G, leaving a little opening for the tulip stem on the right.

9. Appliqué the center tulip next. Add the right tulip, tucking the stem under 1G. Appliqué the little opening on 1G. Trim the background fabric from behind the appliqués.

10. Appliqué the completed background unit to the border circle. Trim the fabric and interfacing from underneath the appliqué, leaving a ¼" seam allowance.

11. Appliqué the circle to the 24" dark background square. Trim the background from behind the appliqué as before. Add the decorative pieces.

Finishing

12. Soak the piece in warm water and remove the freezer paper. When the piece is nearly dry, place it on a towel and use a medium-warm iron to press it dry. Trim the block to 22½" x 22½".

Under the Sea

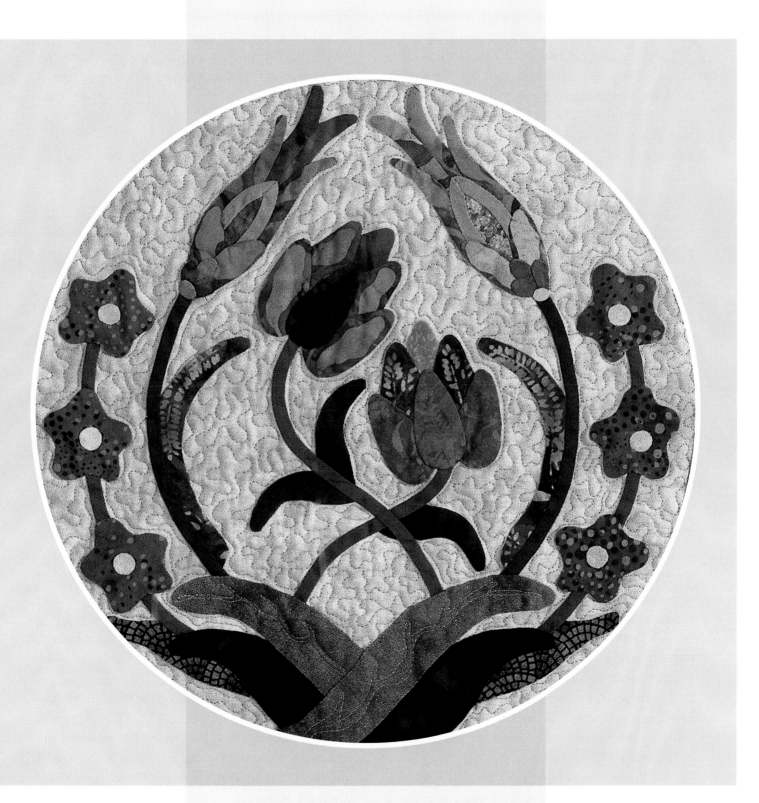

UNDER THE SEA block by Carol A. Hill.
Full quilt shown on page 113.

Under the Sea

was lucky to lift my face to the sunshine and warm breeze of the Golden Horn each day I stayed in Istanbul. The Golden Horn is one of the best natural harbors in our world. Its horn shape naturally divides the European part of Istanbul. There are still homes on the shorelines dating back to the Byzantine and Ottoman eras.

Finished block, 17" x 17"

Fabrics and Supplies

Flowers, stem ring, flowerpot:
  Assorted scraps
Leaves: assorted light, medium,
  and dark scraps
Bias stems: 24" bias tape ¼" wide
  (instructions, page 20)
Light background: 14" x 14"
Circle border: 15" x 15"
Darker background: 19" x 19"
Fusible interfacing:
  14" x 14"
  15" x 15"
Freezer paper: two pieces 14" x 14"

Preparation

Please read the General Instructions, beginning on page 10, before starting your project.

1. To make a master copy, trace the whole pattern (pages 114–117) on the dull side of a 14" freezer-paper square. Turn the master copy over and lightly trace the reversed image on the background square. To make a template copy, trace all the flowers and leaves on the dull side of the other 14" square.

2. On the template copy, add the number-letter labels. Cut the templates apart and press

them, shiny side down, on the backs of the appropriate fabrics.

3. Cut the fabric pieces, adding ³⁄₁₆" turn-under allowances by eye as you cut. Turn the edges that will not be covered by other pieces.

Block assembly

4. Make two flower-1 units, two flower-2 units, six flower-3 units, and one leaf unit, as shown in Fig. 2–29.

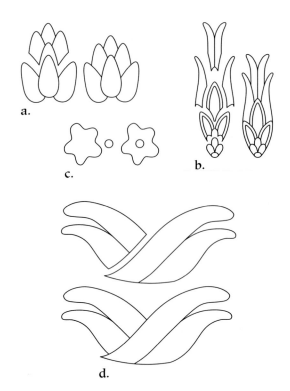

Fig. 2–29. Unit assembly. (a) Flower 1, (b) Flower 2, (c) Flower 3, (d) Leaves.

5. Appliqué the leaves and then the stems for flowers 2 and 3 on the 14" light background square. Add the leaf and stem for flower 1 on the right, then the leaves and stem for flower 1 on the left. Appliqué all the flower units and then the leaf unit.

6. Soak the block in warm water and remove the freezer paper. When the block is nearly dry, place it on a towel and use a medium-warm iron to press it dry.

7. Use the large-circle technique, on page 22, and the 14" fusible-interfacing square to turn the appliquéd square into a 12" circle. In the same manner, use the 15" square of circle border fabric and interfacing to make the 13" border circle.

Finishing

8. Appliqué the 12" circle to the 13" border circle to complete the design. Trim away the interfacings and circle border fabric from underneath the appliqué, leaving ¼" seam allowances.

8. Appliqué the 13" circle to the 19" darker background square. Trim the background from behind the circle, leaving a ¼" seam allowance. Press the block and trim it to 17½" x 17½".

OCEAN BLOOMS, 33½" x 73". Hand appliquéd by Carol A. Hill, Milford, Pennsylvania, and Helen Umstead, Hawley, Pennsylvania; machine quilted by Judy Irish, Arlington, Washington. Three patterns, DANCIN' IN THE MOONLIGHT, WHIRLING TULIPS, and UNDER THE SEA were used to give an exotic peek through a ship's portal for an underwater view of these blooms.

Stems show placement only. A ³⁄₁₆"–¼" stem width is recommended.

Labels within illustration: 2L, 2K, 2M, 2J, 2G, 2F, 2I, 2H, 1C, 1D, 2D, 2C, 2B, 2E, 2A, 2, 1E, circle border, 3, 3A, bias stem, 1C, 1D, 2L, 1B, 1, 1E, 1A, 3A, bias stem

1A
1
1E
2L
3
3A
bias stem
bias stem
bias stem
1R
bias stem
3
3A
4C
bias stem
3R
circle border
4B

Bonus Pattern

Picture Frame

These picture frames are simple, yet they showcase your bouquet to make an exquisite looking piece. You can either appliqué one piece on top of another to achieve a two-toned effect or keep it as one piece. Another option is to use a nice big button in place of appliquéd circle A.

You can use two frames, as in the quilt MOONLIGHT SONATA, on page 123, or use four to accomplish the look of a real framed picture as in GLORIOUS BOUQUET.

GLORIOUS BOUQUET, 21½" x 23½". Hand appliquéd and pieced by the author; machine quilted by Judy Irish, Arlington, Washington. A perfect frame of sage green marbled fabric showcases the woven textured look of the vase.

Half pattern of corner piece.

D

B

A

E

C

THROUGH A TURKISH WINDOW, 32" x 41". Hand appliquéd and hand quilted by Carol A. Hill, Milford, Pennsylvania. Carol has used an arch design, frequently seen in Turkey, to create a window for her bouquet. The quilt is done exclusively in blacks and golds, which coordinate beautifully with the border fabric.

CARNATIONS, 20" x 20". Hand appliquéd and pieced by the author; machine quilted by Judy Irish, Arlington, Washington. Finding a perfect fabric for your border can not only tie all the colors together, but also add some motion and interest.

BLUE SOPHIA, 33" x 46". Hand appliquéd, pieced, and tasseled by Judy Brumbaugh, Milford, Pennsylvania, and machine quilted by Judy Irish, Arlington, Washington. Using the SOPHIA pattern, Judy placed four separate blue tile-like appliqués on cream fabric to give the impression of a banner.

IN REMEMBRANCE, (LEFT), 24½" x 24½". Hand appliquéd and quilted by Nancy S. Morgan, Santa Rosa, California. Using the MEDITERRANEAN MEDALLION pattern, Nancy designed a beautifully embellished arrangement appliquéd on-point in an octagonally shaped quilt.

FANCY TULIPS, 27½" x 27½". Hand appliquéd by the author and her mother, Gloria Grohs, Milford, Pennsylvania; machine quilted by Judy Irish, Arlington, Washington. The centers of each tulip have been selectively cut to display the same design element in each one.

GLORIOUS BOUQUET, 21½" x 23½". Hand appliquéd and pieced by the author's mother, Gloria Grohs; machine quilted by Judy Irish, Arlington, Washington. This vase bursts with fun, colorful stripes. The bouquet is appliquéd within a creamy oval to give the feeling of a cameo brooch.

MY FANCY TULIPS, (RIGHT), 36" x 36". Hand appliquéd and machine pieced by Gloria Grohs, Milford, Pennsylvania; machine quilted by Judy Irish, Arlington, Washington. An embroidered stem stitch was added to enhance the appearance of the marble vase.

FLOWER FRAMES, (LEFT), 40" x 57½". Fancy Tulips block hand appliquéd by Mary Ann Gosch, Shohola, Pennsylvania; Carnations block by Arlene C. Santoro, Shohola, Pennsylvania; Sun Dance block by Susan Leighty, Milford, Pennsylvania. Machine pieced by Susan Caldwell, Westbrookville, New York; machine quilted by Judy Irish, Arlington, Washington.

MY PALACE PURSE, (BOTTOM LEFT), 8" x 14". Hand appliquéd and hand quilted by Leslie Lacika, Milford, Pennsylvania. Half of the SPRING GREEN WREATH pattern was used to create this vibrant little purse. Embellishments have been added to the tips of the flowers, highlighted with stitch work.

KEYS, LIPSTICK AND SPENDING $$, (BOTTOM RIGHT), 11" x 7" purse by JoAnn Musso, Dallas, Texas. This flower appliqué, from the FANCY TULIPS pattern and the leaves and stems from the SPRING GREEN WREATH pattern, was cut from silk and applied with spray adhesive. The appliqués were then free-motion embroidered with rayon thread. (Ghee's Classic Eloquence handbag pattern; see Resources, page 126.)

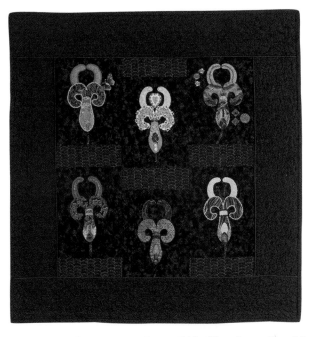

AUGUSTA'S GARDEN, 38" x 40½". Hand appliquéd, pieced, and embellished by the following quilters: Tootsie Schroeder, Irma Stichling, Gloria Grohs, Lillian Angus, Helen Umstead, and Betty Rigo. Machine quilted by Judy Irish.

MOONLIGHT SONATA, 17" x 38". Machine constructed by Bonnie Lyn McCaffery, Hawley, Pennsylvania. This quilt was created with the pattern DANCIN' IN THE MOONLIGHT, using Bonnie's fantasy-fabric technique of capturing things under tulle. The pieces are layered on the background, with tulle added on top, and stitched together with invisible thread. (See Picture Frame pattern on page 118.)

SPIKE'S QUILT, (RIGHT), 23½" x 32". Hand appliquéd and hand quilted by Kathy Oehlmann, Dingmans Ferry, Pennsylvania. Kathy, an artist, hand drew and designed her cat, Spike, as the central focal point of this whimsical quilt.

MEDITERRANEAN MEDALLION, 38" x 51½". Hand appliquéd and pieced by the author; machine quilted by Judy Irish, Arlington, Washington. Hundreds of iridescent pink seed beads were stitched to the lavender medallion piece to give it the appearance of lace. Beautiful crystal gems were attached to the larger flower.

MY TURKISH GARDEN, 90" x 90". Hand appliquéd and hand quilted by Helen Umstead, Hawley, Pennsylvania. Starting in the center with Floral Festivities and progressing with an eclectic and fine-tuned example of each flower, Helen's stitches were like sunshine to the flowers growing in the borders. The final border is finished with a scalloped pattern made with bias tape.

Resources

The Appliqué Society
800 5th Avenue, Suite 101–154
Seattle, WA 98104-3102
E-mail:
    tas@theappliquesociety.org
Website: theappliquesociety.org

Clotilde, Inc.
4301 N. Federal Highway
Ft. Lauderdale, FL 33308
Website: www.clotilde.com
Notions and quilting supplies

Creative Crystals
Lucia Reed
PO Box 1476
Unionville, CT 06085
Phone: 800-578-0716
Website:
    www.creativecrystals.com
Crystal rhinestones, pearls, and metal trims. BeJewler tool (rhinestone applicator)

Bernadine's Needle Arts
For the Creative Embroiderer
Bernie Yoder
244 Tailor Lane
Arthur, IL 61911
Phone: 217-543-2996
Ordering: 888-884-8576
Website:
www.bernadinesneedleart.com
Punch needle kits, silk ribbons, threads, and more

EQuilter
Luana Rubin
4699 Nautilus Ct. South #404
Boulder, CO 80301
Phone: 877-FABRIC 3
Local: 303-527-0856
Customer service:
    service@eQuilter.com
E-mail: luana@eQuilter.com
Website: equilter.com/
Contemporary and ethnic fabrics, books, notions, magazines, patterns, and fabric-related gifts

The Fabric Center
57 Front St.
Pt. Jervis, NY
Phone: 914-856-2122
Fabrics, notions, quilting supplies

Ghee's
Contact: Linda McGhee
2620 Centenary Blvd. #2-250
Shreveport, LA 71104
Phone: 318-226-1701
Phone: 318-226-1781
Website: ghees.com
E-mail: bags@ghees.com
Handbag supplies, vests, garments, and more

Meinke's
Contact: Debra Meinke
724 Sylvanwood
Troy, MI 48098
248-813-9806
http://www.meinketoy.com
E-mail: info@meinketoy.com
Tassels, forms, moulds, tools, cord makers, threads, yarns, books, Shisha mirrors, metallic foils, silks, papermaking supplies, and textile embellishments

Quilter's Attic
P.O. Box 656, Route 302
Pinebush, NY 12566
Phone: 845-744-5888
Website: www.quiltersattic.com
Fabrics, notions, quilting supplies

Timok
PO Box 13161
LaJolla, CA 92039
Phone: 619-677-0740
Website: znet.com/~timok
Tiles and ceramics of Iznik, Turkey

J. T. Trading
Jennifer O'Brien
3 Simm Lane
Newtown, CT 06470
Phone: 203-279-7744
E-mail: order505@aol.com
Website: www.sprayandfix.com
505 basting spray

TravelSmith
60 Leveroni Court
Novato, CA 94949
800-950-1600
Website: www.travelsmith.com
Outfitting guide and catalog for travel gear, including a photographer's vest

Wild Irish Rows
Judy Irish
22826 27th Ave. N.E.
Arlington, WA 98223
Phone: 360-403-4868
E-mail: wildirishrows@yahoo.com
Long-arm machine quilting

The following companies graciously furnished equipment and supplies to help me create this book: Benartex Fabrics, Hoffman Fabrics, J T Trading, Coats & Clark, Clotilde, Clover, Fiskars, Olfa, Mettler, Morgan Hoops and Stands, Creative Crystals.

Bibliography

Akar, Azade. *Treasury of Turkish Designs.* New York: Dover Publications, 1988.

Atasoy, Nurhan, and Julian Raby. *Iznik, The Pottery of Ottoman Turkey.* London, England: Alexandria Press in association with Laurence King, 1994.

The Book of Rustem Pasa Tiles. ed. Fatih Cimok. Istanbul, Turkey: A Turizm Yayinlari, Ltd., Publishers, 1999.

Browning, Bonnie, *Borders & Finishing Touches,* American Quilter's Society, 1998.

Hargrave, Harriet. *Mastering Machine Appliqué.* Lafayette, California: C&T Publishing, 1991.

McCaffery, Bonnie Lyn. *Fantasy Fabrics: Techniques for Layered Surface Design.* Bothell, Washington: Martingale & Co., 1999.

Montano, Judith Baker. *Elegant Stitches.* Lafayette, California: C&T Publishing, 1995.

——. *Floral Stitches.* Lafayette, California: C&T Publishing, 2000.

Pahl, Ellen. *The Quilter's Ultimate Visual Guide.* Emmaus, Pennsylvania: Rodale Press, Inc., 1997.

Pasinli, Alpay, and Saliha Balaman. *Turkish Tiles and Ceramics.* Istanbul, Turkey: A Turizm Yayinlari, Ltd., Publishers, 1991.

Samples, Carole. *Treasury of Crazyquilt Stitches.* Paducah, Kentucky: American Quilter's Society, 1999.

About the Author

Linda M. Poole is a first-generation American. Her father was born in northern Germany on the Denmark border, and her mother is of northern Italian descent. Linda has inherited the good fortune of generations of artists, silversmiths, sculptors, poets, weavers, stained-glass artists, and writers. Her never-ending curiosity about different cultures has given her a passion for travel, teaching, and sharing her experiences with people around the world. Linda has taught in the United States, Italy, Germany, Turkey, and Japan. Language is never a barrier in the translation of quilts.

She lives in a beautiful region on the outskirts of the Pocono Mountains, in Milford, Pennsylvania, overlooking the Delaware River. Living with her are her husband, Bill, and their two "fur-children," Tashi, their loyal canine companion, and Doogin, their kitty, who lazily naps wherever fabric may be.

Other AQS Books

This is only a small selection of the books available from the American Quilter's Society. AQS books are known worldwide for timely topics, clear writing, beautiful color photos, and accurate illustrations and patterns. The following books are available from your local bookseller, quilt shop, or public library.

#6001   us$21.95

#6073   us$19.95

#5855   us$22.95

#5760   us$18.95

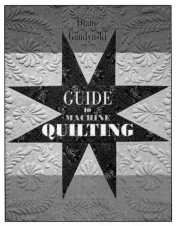

#6070   us$24.95

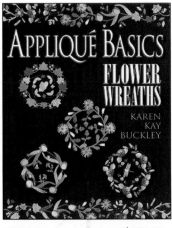

#5335   us$21.95

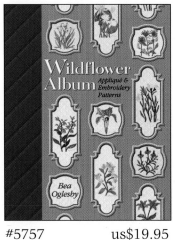

#5757   us$19.95

#5588   us$24.95

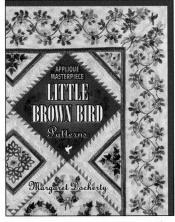

#5338   us$21.95

Look for these books nationally or call 1-800-626-5420